EATING GRASSHOPPERS

EATING GRASSHOPPERS
Chapulines and the Women Who Sell Them

Jeffrey H. Cohen

University of Texas at Austin   *Austin*

Copyright © 2025 by Jeffrey H. Cohen
All rights reserved
Printed in the United States of America
First edition, 2025

Requests for permission to reproduce material from this work should be sent to permissions@utpress.utexas.edu.

♾ The paper used in this book meets the minimum requirements of ANSI/NISO Z39.48–1992 (R1997) (Permanence of Paper).

Library of Congress Cataloging-in-Publication Data

Names: Cohen, Jeffrey H. (Jeffrey Harris), author.
Title: Eating grasshoppers : chapulines and the women who sell them / Jeffrey H. Cohen.
Description: First edition. | Austin : University of Texas at Austin, 2025. | Includes bibliographical references and index.
Identifiers: LCCN 2024047406 (print) LCCN 2024047407 (ebook)
    ISBN 978-1-4773-3227-6 (hardcover)
    ISBN 978-1-4773-3228-3 (paperback)
    ISBN 978-1-4773-3229-0 (pdf)
    ISBN 978-1-4773-3230-6 (epub)
Subjects: LCSH: Entomophagy—Mexico—Oaxaca (State) | Cooking (Insects)—Mexico—Oaxaca (State) | Edible insects—Mexico—Oaxaca (State) | Food habits—Mexico—Oaxaca (State) | Sustainability—Mexico—Oaxaca (State) | Indigenous women—Employment—Mexico—Oaxaca (State) | Rural women—Employment—Mexico—Oaxaca (State) | Businesswomen—Mexico—Oaxaca (State) | Markets—Mexico—Oaxaca (State) | Heritage tourism—Mexico—Oaxaca (State)
Classification: LCC GN409.5 .C64 2025 (print) | LCC GN409.5 (ebook) | DDC 381/.4566495—dc23/eng/20250210
LC record available at https://lccn.loc.gov/2024047406
LC ebook record available at https://lccn.loc.gov/2024047407

doi:10.7560/332276

The University of Texas Press gratefully acknowledges the Pachita Tennant Pike Excellence Endowment for its support of this publication.

For Maria, my love always and forever

CONTENTS

List of Illustrations x
Preface xi

INTRODUCTION. Chapulines, Food, Thought, and Economy 1

PART I. APPROACHING CHAPULINES
CHAPTER 1. Chapulineras: The Women Who Sell Grasshoppers 19
CHAPTER 2. The Harvest and Production 37

PART II. EATING AND THINKING CHAPULINES
CHAPTER 3. Chapulines on the Table 53
CHAPTER 4. The Chapulines Experience 65

PART III. MARKETING CHAPULINES
CHAPTER 5. How to Sell Chapulines in Oaxaca 81
CHAPTER 6. Building a Touchless Economy 95

CONCLUSIONS. Why Chapulines? 107

Acknowledgments 117
Notes 121
References 127
Index 141

ILLUSTRATIONS

FIGURES

Figure 0.1. Chapulines 2
Figure 1.1. Chapulinera, Centro de Abastos, Oaxaca 21
Figure 2.1. Chapulinera in her restaurant, Mitla, Oaxaca 39
Figure 2.2. Preparation of chapulines 46
Figure 2.3. Chapulinera, Sunday market, Tlacolula 49
Figure 3.1. Chapulinera, *panadería* (bakery), Mercado Zimatlán, Zimatlán, Oaxaca 54
Figure 3.2. Chapulinera, Tlacolula, Chapulines *en venta* (for sale) 62
Figure 5.1. An entrepreneur and third-generation chapulinera, Mercado 20 de Noviembre, Oaxaca 89
Figure C.1. Sister chapulineras and entrepreneurs, Mercado 20 de Noviembre, Oaxaca 114

TABLES

Table 1.1. Chapulinera Hometowns, 2022 Field Season 27
Table 1.2. Marginality Scale, 2020 33
Table 3.1. Typical Meals for Rural Oaxacan Families, 2008 59
Table 4.1. Chapulineras' Control over Sales of Chapulines 73
Table 5.1. Weekly Sales by Chapulineras, Summer 2022 88
Table 5.2. Who Collects Chapulines 91
Table 5.3. Where Chapulines Are Collected 92
Table 5.4. Sales in Addition to Chapulines 94

PREFACE

MY FIRST ENCOUNTER WITH CHAPULINES was during an early visit to Oaxaca. I was attending a Spanish immersion program in the city and renting a room from a family living in the Lomas del Crestón neighborhood. The family was Zapotec and from the eastern branch of the central valleys. They used their city home as a base for their children to attend the Universidad Autónoma Benito Juárez de Oaxaca (UABJO). Most Friday afternoons we would catch a bus heading out of the city to spend the weekend in their home village.

There was always a bowl of chapulines on the kitchen table. For me, that bowl was unexpected. I had never tried an insect and had not thought about eating grasshoppers—regardless of their preparation. Nevertheless, my hosts would tease me, holding them up, palm open: "Gringo, they are high in protein," or, "Gringo, they are low in calories!" They clearly had a sense of what mattered for a health-conscious foreigner, but I was not ready to try an insect, even if it was edible. This went on for several weekends, and we would typically end with whoever was leading the discussion eating the chapulines they were holding with a flourish and a sigh of contentment. I did finally work up the courage to try one, and that stopped the taunting. Eating a grasshopper was not easy, but I closed my eyes, thought about something else, and took a bite. Chapulines might not be something I had been ready to eat, and they certainly were not my first choice for a snack, but they weren't terrible.

A few years later I was living in Santa Ana del Valle with my wife, Maria. Santa Ana is a small Zapotec community built around family farming, the artisanal production of *tapetes* (woolen rugs), and a growing reliance on transnational migration (Cohen 1999, 2004b). One early morning in October, I drove with Don Mauro (my patron and sponsor) into the foothills of the mountains that rose to the north of our village. We were harvesting *cempasúchiles* (marigolds) to decorate altars for Día de Los Muertos (Day of the Dead) and gathering firewood. After about an hour of collecting, we took a break; Don Mauro pulled a bag of chapulines and tortillas from his pack. As we were sitting together and looking over the valley stretched below us, he made a taco, rolling a tortilla around a handful of chapulines. He handed me one without saying a word. I accepted the taco without complaint and took a bite. Don Mauro nodded as he acknowledged what was, for me, a big deal. Rested and fed, we returned to our work, heading home after another hour or so with a trunkload of flowers and firewood and in time to enjoy a proper breakfast.

Chapulines are found throughout Oaxaca's markets, including the Mercado Benito Juárez near the Zócalo, in the city's center. Chapulineras (the women who prepare and sell chapulines) sit among vendors selling so much stuff and speaking so many different languages that it can be overwhelming.[1] I was at a loss to describe the market during my early visits, and even though I am now armed with experience of the place, it can still seem like controlled chaos. Wandering the aisles after years of research, I still find my attention drawn this way and that, whether I am visiting the Centro de Abastos (the major market for the city), a zonal, neighborhood market like El Mercado la Merced, or a regional weekly market like the Sunday market in Tlacolula. The mix of new and old; the noise; and the foods, produce, treats, and smells are overwhelming, inviting, and lingering.

The marketplace can seem chaotic; nevertheless, there is a pattern to the chaos. Stalls are organized around shared themes, and while the combinations of foods can be unexpected, the logic of the layout is clear. Vendors are clustered according to goods. In one section, there are stalls filled with fruits, vegetables, cheese, and chapulines. The chapulines—cooked, red, and inviting—are ready to sell. Chapulineras have regular clients who buy by the kilogram weekly. For most outsiders and non-Oaxacans, it can be hard to appreciate just how much will sell, how popular chapulines are, and how much money changes hands. Chapulines are unique; they do not look or smell like anything most non-Oaxacans have seen or eaten. In fact, for most Westerners, edible insects are not a thing. They are a food source that does not fit our expectations and falls well outside the boundaries of palatability (La Barbera et al. 2018; Wade 2021). Nevertheless, in Oaxaca, they cannot be missed.

Chapulines are one of hundreds of different insects consumed in Mexico (Gallardo-López et al. 2023; Ramírez-Arriaga et al. 2011; Ramos-Elorduy 1997). Alongside fruits, chapulineras sell strings of *gusanos* (worms, or, more accurately, the larvae of beetles that burrow into agave cactus), *chicatanas* (flying ants), and *sal de gusano* (a combination of salt, chiles, and *gusanos* ground together into a pungent umber-colored seasoning).

Tasting chapulines can be a real challenge. And it takes time to work up the nerve to try a bite. Though I first tried chapulines many years ago, it wasn't something I was ready to eat every day. I started with a sample here and a nibble there. In the market, I would randomly pick a chapulinera and ask whether I might try a sample or purchase a small bag. Encouraging me, the chapulinera typically offered a bite. I learned to enjoy them, and, in the process, I developed this project.

Chapulineras are talented businesswomen. They know how to engage with their clients as well as gringo anthropologists. They know how to make a sale, and they were kind enough to talk with me and my research team during fieldwork that started in 2006 and continued with additional visits in 2007, 2008, and 2021–2023. Chapulineras shared their stories, experiences, hopes, and dreams. They taught me how to properly eat chapulines (skip the legs, as they can scratch your throat) and shared stories of how they came to create their businesses, how they manage production, and how they succeed.

Chapulines are a seasonal treat, but they are not for everyone. Researchers argue that eating edible insects is nearly impossible for people who have not grown up with them on the menu (Pali-Schöll et al. 2019). In fact, entomophagy (eating insects) can carry a consumer beyond disgust and cause them to vomit (Kosonen 2022; MacClancy et al. 2009). And yet, it is hard to say no when offered chapulines. Putting aside assumptions about what is edible, it is worth trying chapulines (Messer 2007). Whether I was hauling firewood and collecting *cempasúchiles* or conducting fieldwork, if I was hungry and the only thing available were chapulines, I ate them.

Chapulines do not taste as you might expect. They have a unique flavor with a strong note of the garlic and *limón* (lime) that they are cooked in, as well as a slight aftertaste. But the most disconcerting part of eating chapulines for most everyone outside of Oaxaca is the fact that you have eaten an insect.[2] Oaxacans say, "If you eat a *chapulín*, you will return to Oaxaca." It is a funny saying to share. But if the experience goes well, you might decide to buy a small bag to eat later.

Oaxacans are not exceptional in their love of chapulines. Entomophagy is common in Mexico and around the world (Ramos-Elorduy 1997). Edible insects have been a part of the Mexican diet for thousands of years. They were a critical protein source for pre-Columbian peoples and remained important during the colonial and postcolonial periods. Today, insects continue to be a popular food, and when they are in season (from the arrival of May's rains through the late autumn), Oaxacans are happy to choose chapulines in place of other foods that might seem more appealing to outsiders.

I have worked in the central valleys of Oaxaca for decades. Inspired by Elsie Clews Parsons (1936), who conducted fieldwork in Mitla (a historically important community in the eastern branch of the central valleys) in the early twentieth century, my first efforts were to document how Indigenous Oaxacans responded to increasing globalization and the impacts of things like the 1992 North American Free Trade Agreement (NAFTA) (Cohen 2001). Later, I focused on transnational migration and remittance practices from the perspective of sending communities to document how folks made sense of, organized, and adapted to migration (Cohen 2004b). In these projects I was not thinking about chapulines, but I was eating them, and they occasionally showed up on my plate.

A presence on many kitchen tables, chapulines are valuable, and the women who sell them make good money. That women can earn well selling chapulines becomes even more important in light of the limited opportunities for work in rural Oaxaca. In addition to their importance on local tables, chapulines have shown up on menus throughout Oaxaca, in other parts of Mexico, and in the United States. You can find them in local Mexican food stores sold by the kilo, in restaurants served with mezcal, and at Mariners baseball games in Seattle alongside more traditional ballpark treats. Putting together my experiences and referencing the market value of chapulines for the women who sell them, I organized this study.

— INTRODUCTION —
CHAPULINES, FOOD, THOUGHT, AND ECONOMY

Oaxacans do not always eat chapulines, but when they do they describe them as delicious. Chapulines are a satisfying and tasty treat. To paraphrase Señora Olivia Melchor, a chapulinera who sells in the Mercado 20 de Noviembre (November 20 Market), chapulines are like peanuts: easy to carry and easy to eat.[1] They are also a healthy choice, and chapulineras describe them as a fresh, clean, and satisfying source of protein.

Doña Paola Guzmán, a chapulinera from Zimatlán (interviewed in 2008), contrasted chapulines, which are harvested from local fields of *maíz* (corn) and alfalfa, with meat proteins, which are bought from butchers who may not know their provenience. She declared, "There is no reason not to eat grasshoppers [chapulines]. . . . They are natural compared to meats, which are not good to eat because they [stock animals] eat anything and bring diseases that can affect people's health."[2]

Most Oaxacans are familiar with chapulines (figure 0.1). They know how to eat them and recognize their nutritional value. They are also aware that chapulines have been a part of the diet dating to pre-Columbian times. Nevertheless, contemporary consumption is not a holdover. No one eats chapulines because tradition and history dictate that they must; in fact, the changing nature of the diet might suggest a declining interest in edible insects as other foods and choices take their place. Yet locals continue to purchase and eat them in a way that parallels the arrival of any seasonal specialty (Aigbedion-Atalor et al. 2024; Pérez-Lloréns 2024).

FIGURE 0.1. *Chapulines. Photo by author.*

Grown, harvested, and cooked locally, chapulines are ubiquitous and found in kitchens and on tables throughout Oaxaca's central valleys. They are a practical choice, and people are happy to snack on them throughout the day. The chapulines season begins with the arrival of spring rains in May and continues through mid-fall, following a pattern associated with Oaxaca's geographic location in the tropics (Magaña et al. 1999).

Chapulines are a regular part of everyday life. They are consumed as a quick bite while working, a before-breakfast jolt of energy, or a snack between meals that is rolled into tortillas with a dash of salsa. Consumption is not limited to rural and indigenous Oaxacans. Urban folks living in Oaxaca City as well as surrounding centers like Tlacolula and Zimatlán share a love for chapulines that is clear in the excitement that greets their arrival and the mountains of chapulines that are available in the marketplace. There is almost always a bag of chapulines to snack on in most city homes.

A delicious, welcome, and beloved treat, chapulines are also a symbol of Indigenous stability and rural survival over time. Chapulines as a regular and reoccurring food that has been shared over time serve as a counternarrative to the stories of poverty and the painful history of inequality associated with Indigenous and rural life in Oaxaca (Ramos-Elorduy 2009). In a sense, eating chapulines is a declaration of independence and freedom from the state and a rejection of the state's condemnation of entomophagy as backward and ill-fitting for modern-day peoples (Hurd et al. 2019). Chapulines are a natural food, and both local growers and chapulineras are quick to defend their value and purity, despite concerns over lead contamination (Handley et al. 2007).[3]

Chapulines have been part of the Oaxacan kitchen for many generations, and entomophagy has deep roots in the region's pre-Columbian past. Nevertheless, it is wrong to describe the historical (or prehistoric) practice of entomophagy as somehow critical to eating chapulines in the present. Eating chapulines has always been a choice; while there may have been unique factors that framed that choice in the past (for example, the lack of beef on the Mesoamerican menu until the arrival of the Spanish), there were always options (Staller and Carrasco 2010). In addition to small game, fowl, and fish, there were many insects available for consumption, including *jumiles* (stink bugs), *chicatanas*, *ahuatle* (water bugs and water bug eggs), *gusanos* (worms or larvae), and *escamoles* (ant eggs or ant roe), as well as insect by-products including honey (Ramos-Elorduy 1997, 2009).

"The use of insects in Mexican cuisine is tenacious and enduring" (Castañón 2021, 255) and the consumption of chapulines may have its roots in ancient traditions and practices that developed around the foodways of pre-Columbian peoples, but contemporary consumption is not founded on those traditions. The changing foodscapes that came with the Spanish conquest meant the introduction of new crops, animals, and dietary rules that defined entomophagy and the consumption of any insect to be barbaric (see the discussions in Gregorio 2021; Wylie 2006). Nevertheless, many tour guides and restauranteurs interpret pre-Columbian history and pair the consumption of chapulines with fantastic stories of Oaxaca's Indigenous peoples to create a direct connection between past and present (see, e.g., Oaxaca Auténtico, n.d.; Olano 2020). The stories portray an idyllic Indigenous world defined by plenty, celebrated as safe, and marked by a balanced, humane approach to living. Chapulines are one of the foods—along with tortillas, mole, and a few other regional specialties—used to tell the story of a place that exists outside the forces of capitalism, alien to the surrounding nation and remaining unchanged through both colonial and contemporary times. Identified as Indigenous, such stories create a world that is scrubbed of controversy, lacks structural inequalities, and is uncontaminated, pure, and bucolic. Ignoring the complex history of the region both before and after the arrival of the Spanish and during Mexico's growth as a nation creates an image of Oaxacans and chapulineras as humble and engaged in the production of a food that is founded in a glorious past (Stephen 1991, 22).

The misreading of history and the assumption that contemporary foodways emerged unchanged from past practices make it difficult to understand how choices were made in the past and how those choices have changed in the present. Chapulines were always a choice; there was always something else to eat. The choices Oaxacans made changed with the arrival of Spain (Bérubé and Forde 2024). Once the region had become a colony, demand for new crops and new animal proteins, as well as the pressures that the growth of these new crops and support of new animals had on local communities, upended norms of the time. These forces changed what were recognized and sanctioned foodways that were critical to the local population. The shifting dynamics of food production and new ways of eating imposed new assumptions about race and Indigeneity that tended to disparage Indigenous foods and marginalize traditional choices.

Simply put, while contemporary Oaxacans may eat some of the same foods that their ancestors consumed, they do not think of them in the same ways or eat them for the same reasons. The change in consumption is more than a historical shift in food practices. Over the last several decades chapulines have been transformed from a largely ignored, overlooked, and unimportant food consumed by the rural, urban, and Indigenous poor, into a delicacy and must-have taste for visitors to the city. For outsiders, chapulines have gone from unappetizing and inedible insects to part of the city's haute cuisine (Sammells 2019).

Chapulines are presented as a part of the state's Indigenous heritage and a powerful symbol of Oaxaca, alongside other local specialties such as mole and mezcal (Brulotte and Starkman 2013; Cohen, Mata-Sánchez, et al. 2009; Friedensohn 2001; Hernández Ramírez 2023). And yet, while outsiders' demand for chapulines grows, their interest remains of minor importance to chapulineras. The sales made to outsiders and restauranteurs are limited, and they are, particularly where tourists are concerned, generally one-offs—in contrast with the hundreds of kilograms of prepared grasshoppers that chapulineras move weekly.[4]

While chapulineras focus most of their energies on the local market and local clientele, they understand that chapulines have become a powerful symbol of Oaxaca that is celebrated as a unique treat. Eating chapulines is part of the way in which people enact local identity, vie for attention and relevance, rethink the history of the state, and engage with larger systems of power. But whereas the relationships that visitors construct through chapulines speak to a fictional past that is expressed as a commitment to native traditions (Hernández-Rojas and Huete Alcocer 2021), the relationships that Oaxacans create through chapulines reflect the everyday, and what Alan Warde (2016) and Richard Wilk (2004) describe as the mundane act of eating. The complexity of the moment is not lost on chapulineras, who are happy to exploit an assumed connection to an authentic Oaxaca, even if the sales are limited.

More than food, chapulines are motifs and mascots associated with businesses in Mexico and the United States.[5] *Alebrijes*, brightly painted wooden animals and fantasy-inspired carvings sold in city galleries and produced in the nearby towns of Atzompa and San Martín Tilcajete, often feature chapulines as their subject. They are the namesake of the local Chapulineros soccer squad and are highlighted throughout the city of Oaxaca and beyond, in association with taxis, buses, hotels, and restaurants. Chapulines are a regular part of many different celebrations, and vendors bring them out, with other street foods, packaged in bags or wrapped in newspaper to be consumed like popcorn.

The symbolism of chapulines is not always celebratory. Chapulines are also associated with inequality, ecological disaster, and hardship. During the COVID-19 pandemic, chapulines were an important protein source, particularly when families were unable to access meats. The reliance of families on chapulines recalls periods of drought and conflicts in the seventeenth and eighteenth centuries and emphasizes the challenges associated with rural poverty, social inequality, and the assumption that edible insects are a crisis food (see also Endfield et al. 2004).

Chapulines are a good source of protein, and in a disaster, they will often be consumed when other forms of protein are not as easily accessible. The use of chapulines can also differentiate those who have resources and access to aid from those who are lacking support. When faced with a crisis, the rural poor typically have nowhere to turn and rely on what is available. Often what is available when a family needs a consistent form of protein are chapulines (Martínez-Martínez et al. 2023). The complexity of meanings and uses will always mark chapulines as symbols, as an everyday food, and as a food of last resort. Nevertheless, the speculative abstractions of visitors to the city will vie with the more complex and concrete views of locals in the creation of meaning (Sammells 2024).

Tourists and foodies define chapulines as part of Mexico's Indigenous history, though they are often following guidebooks and social media sites rather than academic research.[6] Chapulines, celebrated as an Indigenous delicacy and one of many insects consumed in Mesoamerica, become an iconic marker of the pre-Columbian past. Entomophagy is off-putting and alien for most visitors to Oaxaca. Eating bugs is simply not done. Chapulines are presented to outsiders and used to make sense of what can seem alien (and alienating). The stories that popular sites and cookbooks promote connect the consumption of chapulines by locals to the food's historical presence and place in pre-Columbian life. In other words, they infer that entomophagy happens because that is what the region's ancestors did. This framework for thinking about chapulines contrasts with that of locals who approach edible insects as food. Chapulines may represent seasonality, time, belonging, and celebration, but, fundamentally, they are practical and their regular consumption is part of everyday life. For locals, chapulines satisfy natural, biological, and social needs (Warde 2016; Wilk 2004).

Chapulines are a choice, but they are not the only choice. There is almost always something else to eat. Nevertheless, for locals, chapulines have always been on the table and always available to them. Adults remember eating chapulines as youngsters; young Oaxacans shake with glee and anticipation as the season starts and the first fresh toasted chapulines come off the comal (a ceramic or metal griddle and cooking surface). Outsiders can also choose to eat chapulines. And the many forms they can take, from snack to main dish, are beyond the imagination of most nonlocal consumers.

Chapulines can be a challenge for outsiders and visitors to the state, and their consumption is often approached with trepidation and disgust. Chapulines are inedible insects for most outsiders (Lesnik 2019). To counter the negative reaction and to moderate the "yuck" response that comes with eating an insect, chapulines are presented as part of the Indigenous diet, a neat dare, and a symbol of the consumer's status as a boundary breaker. Whether chapulines are approached as an opportunity to "eat like an Indian," a dare, or a status builder, they are special, and along with mezcal they have come to define Oaxaca and Oaxacan cuisine, and are increasingly a "must try."[7]

Chapulines are both more and less than grasshoppers. *Saltamontes* (Spanish for grasshoppers in general) are not exactly chapulines. *Saltamontes* identifies all grasshoppers; in Oaxaca, it is often applied to larger grasshoppers that are not collected, toasted, or eaten. In fact, *saltamontes* are a nuisance or pest, while chapulines are a delicacy. Sometimes chapulines are confused with crickets, and in the US products that include crickets as an ingredient are often labeled with a name that plays on the term *chapulín*. Nevertheless, locals do not eat and do not collect or cook crickets. Most Oaxacans describe crickets as disgusting, inedible, and strange. Where chapulines are a crunchy, savory treat, crickets are bitter and mealy, and they carry a lingering, metallic aftertaste.

To outsiders and non-Mexicans, chapulines are exceptional, an artifact of a lost past. In light of their connection to Oaxaca's Indigenous past and the foods of pre-Columbian peoples, it is easy to assume that chapulines hold special meaning as cultural symbols in the present (Ahamed-Broadhurst, n.d.). Misreading the meaning of chapulines can be useful for outsiders and non-Mexicans as they experience edible insects. Their choice has to do less with chapulines as food and more with their assumed embodiment of a pre-Columbian past and a time before the introduction of alternatives by the Spanish Crown.

While the stories of ancient traditions can enhance the meaning, spirituality, and value of chapulines for outsiders, they remain an everyday part of a meal for locals. They are not something to celebrate but instead something to be rolled into a taco or eaten by the handful. The difference in the use of chapulines is critical. They are an exceptionally good way for locals to satisfy hunger, particularly between meals and when hard at work. That does not take away from their status as a symbol or their role for outsiders who are looking for an experience and connection to the past. However, the difference between local and outsider does give rise to an awkward dynamic in terms of contested meanings, status, and value (Wilk 2006). While the former is focused on eating and satisfying a need, the latter is thinking about the past, the present, and, of course, the fact that an insect is about to pass their lips.

The role of chapulines in Oaxaca has changed through time. What pre-Columbian folks ate was not the same as what Oaxacans consumed following the conquest, and today's consumers continue to create their own unique stories.

Complicating how the stories of chapulines are told is the fact that they were a disaster food for generations of Oaxacans, who turned to them when other foods were not available (Endfield et al. 2004). Drought, earthquakes, and warfare were all factors that drove consumption. During data collection for my first major study in the area (see Cohen 1999), older Santañeros (the people of the village of Santa Ana del Valle, Oaxaca) talked about eating chapulines, among other things, as their fields and crops were burned during the Mexican Revolution. The challenges of those times were reawakened by the COVID-19 pandemic, when chapulines again became an effective source of protein for families that were isolated in their home villages and cut off from local markets (Cohen and Mata-Sánchez 2021).

From humble beginnings, chapulines are featured by state tourism and presented as a critical part of the food traditions that make Oaxaca special. Foodies have descended on the city, and no trip is complete without at least a taste of chapulines. Chapulines are served with mezcal; in fact, a plate of chapulines is often followed with a shot of mezcal to create a unique and ostensibly Indigenous experience. Chapulines are part of the definition of Oaxaca as a culinary hot spot (see Alaniz 2011; Weslander 2019). They reflect the past and Indigenous foodways, and, through new sorts of preparations, they become a part of a cosmopolitan future. While it might seem difficult to persuade tourists and outsiders to try an edible insect, the dare culture that has developed around their consumption helps. By facilitating eating of the past and participation in traditions, chapulines allow outsiders to become Oaxacan, even if only for the briefest moment.

The role chapulines play as cultural symbols for tourists and foodies is quite different from their importance to chapulineras and their economic well-being. Chapulines are at the center of a vibrant and active market that reaches well beyond the state. Chapulineras sell to locals and regularly ship to the United States, where chapulines are available in small grocery stores, *tiendas* (shops), and restaurants.

The market for chapulines is vital and vibrant. Yet unlike the markets that have developed around mezcal, crafts, clothing, and art, which tend to be controlled by external investments (Lira et al. 2022), the market for chapulines is dominated by local women. Outside investors are not invited to join or to become involved in production and sales, and chapulineras do not take loans or affiliate with development programs. Chapulineras are not interested in bringing in market specialists, and nearly everyone we interviewed voiced fear of NGO promoters and development specialists focused on increasing sales.

While tourism dominates business in Oaxaca, chapulineras are generally disinterested in selling directly to tourists, working with tour guides, or tailoring their pitch to outsiders. The sales that can be made to tourists and foodies are simply too small. Chapulineras report that very little money comes from outsiders. Outsiders buy only a small amount of chapulines and typically make only one purchase during their visit. In other words, sales to tourists and foodies are a small bonus that comes in addition to regular sales. The sales that matter and that keep the market going come from the hundreds of kilograms that are sold locally.

The local control of the market that chapulineras exercise, and the limited impact of tourist sales, contrasts with the production of mezcal and a multitude of crafts. Alyshia Gálvez (2018), writing on the impacts of the 1992 North American Free Trade Agreement (NAFTA) on food in Mexico, notes that external investments in tourism generally benefit only big (and often foreign) investors, leaving local communities with little to show. In other words, the local gains that are often promised as a product of increasing tourism are largely ephemeral, as profits flow out of the region and into the hands of foreign interests (Wilson 2008). But the market for chapulines is quite unique, and chapulineras do not depend on external investments, leaving profits to local producers, whose hard work pays off and is evident in their earnings and dominance of the marketplace.

The harvest and preparation of chapulines for sale follows a cycle of production that begins with the arrival of the spring rains and the appearance of grasshoppers in milpas (gardens) and alfalfa fields throughout the central valleys. The income that women can generate through selling chapulines during the season can be substantial. It allows their children to complete school and attend college; creates the opportunity to buy consumables, including foods, large appliances, and cars; and covers the costs of health care and home renovations, often including the installation of access to piped water and Western-style bathrooms.

The women who sell chapulines are skilled in managing production and sales. Whether they are in the marketplace or at home, it is common to see them on their mobile phones, working nonstop with their suppliers and clientele. Several women noted that their best customers are from their extended families, hometowns, and nearby villages. Nevertheless, their efforts are not underwritten by a morality that demands special treatment for family and friends. Chapulineras are focused on their business. They recognize that the most important goal is to make sales, earn profits, and invest their earnings in themselves and their children. Anthropologists often characterize the Indigenous as victims of progress who are unable to adapt to the expanding global markets around them, unable to embrace new technologies, and incapable of adapting to a changing world. The argument often paints Indigenous communities as facing certain trouble, destined to become part of the rural poor or the lumpen proletariat, and doomed to lose the very traditions that made them unique in the past.

Nothing could be further from reality for the women who sell chapulines in Oaxaca. Though many of these women are poor, their heritage does not consign them to poverty (and see Cohen et al. 2009; Forte, n.d.). What is exceptional are the ways in which these women adapt and adjust, whether that means adding a few sales to restauranteurs and tourists or inventing a touchless economy to facilitate the movement of hundreds of kilograms of products while coping with a pandemic that threatens access to food and, in the process, everyone's well-being and health.

The story of chapulines in Oaxaca is really the story of the women who produce and sell them from their homes and in the marketplace. From harvest to production and from selling at home to exporting across the US border, each stage of the story brings its own importance and values, and even a few surprises.

PART I. APPROACHING CHAPULINES

Chapulines and entomophagy: the insect and the act of eating the insect. Grasshoppers are not new to the world and are identifiable during the early Triassic period, around 250 million years ago. Today, grasshoppers are dispersed globally and include over 6,700 unique species (Song et al. 2018).

Entomophagy appeared when the first bug was consumed. Eating insects was critical to hominin evolution, and insects have continued to be an important protein source for humans through time (Lesnik 2018; Liceaga 2022; van Huis 2017). Nevertheless, grasshoppers from the past are not chapulines today, and chapulines today are not ancient artifacts of a foodway that dates to early human evolution. Part I (chapters 1 and 2) focuses on chapulines as a modern food as well as their importance for consumers and chapulineras.

Humans are omnivores; we can and do eat nearly everything. For this reason, entomophagy must be measured alongside the opportunity to eat lots of other things. The omnivore's dilemma, or the burden of choice that weighs on eaters as they select what to eat and what to avoid (Alt et al. 2022; Armelagos 2014), might seem simpler in our species' deep history or Oaxaca's pre-Columbian past. But that assumption reflects our bias and entomophobia; it disregards the ways that eating habits change in response to new foods and technologies, as well as the introduction of new crops and stock animals. The bias against entomophagy in the West also influences how we respond to its practice and reflects an assumption that people who consume edible insects do so only when there are no other foods available. The reality is that our diet has changed again and again, and the traditions of entomophagy practiced in the deep past were unique and have been replaced time and time again as systems and cultures have changed.

Throughout the colonial period, rural and Indigenous peoples found their everyday patterns of consumption and eating challenged, disparaged, and upended by new and powerful foodways that highlighted European tastes and practices. The challenges around eating continued into the twentieth century, as the Mexican state worked to replace Indigenous food practices, even seeking to limit the tortilla based on an argument that bread would lift Indigenous communities out of poverty (Ochoa 2000). New foods, including Spanish proteins and grains, competed with and often displaced local fare. Yet colonial controls and Spanish demands reproduced social hierarchies that limited access to many of these newly introduced foods and foreign ways of eating for local populations. In some instances, native populations were tasked with the care of these new crops and animals but never given the opportunity to partake of them (Rudra and Tobin 2017).

Nearly two billion people continue to consume insects globally (van Huis et al. 2022). Nevertheless, the food landscape has shifted over time, and even as many people continue to consume insects, there are always alternatives. Some alternatives are rich in proteins, others not so much. The choice is complicated, and the dilemma is real. Edible insects, even when they are included on the plate or listed on the menu, are no longer a core food whose centrality in the diet comes from their critical role as a recognized and accepted protein.

PART II. EATING AND THINKING CHAPULINES

Part I defines the importance of chapulines as food, as well as the role of the women who sell them. Nevertheless, food is about more than energy and eating, and few people would say that they choose a meal for its nutritional or caloric status alone. Part II (chapters 3 and 4) explores how the food choices humans make are informed by a series of factors including cultural ideas concerning what is good, edible, and safe; what is off-putting; what is healthy or unhealthy; and what other people are eating.

Thinking about chapulines gives eaters, native and otherwise, an opportunity to consider reality and dream of new relationships that combine a misreading of empirical observations (there are chapulines) with speculative abstractions about history (chapulines are an Indigenous delicacy) and in the process reinvent their place in the cultural worlds we create (Di Giovine and Brulotte 2013; Lévi-Strauss 1963). Chapulines have diverse meanings for different kinds of eaters and in different kinds of settings. Sometimes their meanings are contradictory to reality (as when they are used to frame a mythological Oaxaca that has little to do with the struggles and conflicts faced by its Indigenous and rural poor) or simply negative (as when the flavors of the past are rejected by younger eaters) (Friedensohn 2001; Hernández Ramírez 2023).

Yet other meanings abound. Most often chapulines are a tradition welcomed by Oaxacans, a comfort food that brings a smile to a consumer's face. But they are also a crisis food; through time, eating chapulines has come to be associated with famine, disasters, and, most recently, the COVID-19 pandemic. To outsiders, chapulines are a dare, an opportunity to eat an insect, and a chance to eat like "an ancestor" and to prove one's mettle (Berger et al. 2018; Legendre and Baker 2021). For others, chapulines are part of a moral alternative that is critical to the future of our planet and to the reduction of harmful greenhouse gases, climate change, and an overreliance on beef (van Huis et al. 2013). The dynamic play of these opposing meanings and values places chapulines at the center of ongoing debates (Cohen and Schuster 2019).

PART III. MARKETING CHAPULINES

More than food and more than culture, part III (chapters 5 and 6) explores the value and meaning of chapulines for the women who harvest, process, and sell them. Chapulines are a business, and understanding the chapulines business is critical to understanding the place of entomophagy in rural Oaxacan life. By following the grasshopper life cycle, we can appreciate how chapulines have become critical to the local diet. By tracing the cycle of production, we can comprehend their economic importance in the life of the Oaxacan family.

The business of selling chapulines is straightforward. It is a system that is defined by supply and demand. Nevertheless, understanding how rural Oaxacan women turn this system into a comfortable living is a story worth telling. Chapulines are a big business, and chapulineras are serious, hardworking, and innovative. They are also exhausted, stressed, and happy to make sales that will cover everyday expenses, new opportunities for their children, and more. They are in constant motion as they shift between their roles as businesswomen, mothers, sisters, and wives.

Arguably, the most important innovation for chapulineras over the last decade (since the 2010s) has been their growing reliance on cell phone technology and the use of social media to connect with new clientele. In 2020 chapulineras began to organize a touchless economy to cope with market closures brought on by the pandemic. But the economics of chapulines reach well beyond Oaxaca's market system. In fact, many of the women we interviewed are involved in the local marketplace and the export market. Some use social media sites to meet new clients, and many participate in contracts that find them shipping chapulines across the US-Mexico border and to destinations across North America.

What can chapulines teach us about food anthropology? The assumption that toasted grasshoppers are part of a traditional diet that is rooted in the pre-Columbian past and informed by an almost genetically defined passion reflects the earliest forays of anthropologists into a discussion of food. While early work in and around anthropology recognized the breadth of what humans could eat, including insects, the process of documenting what humans ate often played out as an exercise in comparative studies that focused less on the foods eaten and more on the ways those foods differed. A parallel line of thinking views entomophagy as chiefly about survival (Gahukar 2011): What mattered was not taste or tradition, but the calories and the protein. Writing for the website Culinary Backstreets, María Ítaka (2021) notes the utilitarian value of chapulines: "Before the Spanish brought cattle, the original inhabitants of Mexico got their protein mainly from ducks, turkeys, wild pigs, fish and different kinds of insects."

Chapulines are an exceptional protein source. Nevertheless, the ancestors of today's Oaxacans were not calculating protein content or counting calories. They were eating, telling stories about what and how they ate, and making careful decisions about what they might eat. While the food available might not have included as many variations as are found in the present (a time when eaters can choose from hundreds of possibilities that range from freshly harvested to store-bought and packaged), chapulines were only one of many foods available to them. There were other insects and many alternatives for consumption, although those alternatives were limited by the ecology and history of the region (postcolonial foods, introduced by the Spanish and others, had not yet appeared).

To assume that contemporary Oaxacans consume chapulines due to predisposition is to reduce the population to machines following a deeply rooted, nearly genetic drive. This robs them of the ability to make decisions, falsely suggesting that one food or a small suite of foods represents consumption through time and that adaptation (in this case, to introduced crops like wheat and alfalfa and new proteins that include cattle) takes place only under duress. Reality is far more complicated and is, as George J. Armelagos (2014) notes, adaptive, sensorial, and cultural.

By limiting the ability of the individual to make decisions, we also limit our own ability to understand how the dynamics of food choice play out in space and time, how food comes to be "thought," and how the consumption of chapulines changes in response to new ways of eating. Finally, by ignoring the ways Oaxacans adapt to new foodways and create opportunities, we lose the chance to understand how chapulines become the basis for a booming economy in the present.

CONCLUSION

Chapulines are more than grasshoppers, and chapulineras sell more than food. They sell culture, and they do so in a world in which they are marginalized and maligned. Rooted in the deep past and revised following the conquest, their marginality is expressed in their systematic impoverishment, regardless of the profits they make in the marketplace. Studying the consumption and sales of chapulines is an opportunity to follow how local folks eat, adapt, and find opportunities. It is also a chance to learn how food and its meaning change through time. Understanding the process is not about converting chapulineras into political heroes who lead a fight against the penetration of premade and prepackaged foods, or about lamenting the rise of tourism and arrival of foodies who co-opt local traditions. Rather, chapulines are the lens through which we can understand chapulineras' success and the way that the invention of pre-Columbian eating by outsiders misrepresents their changing value and meaning.

— PART I —
APPROACHING CHAPULINES

--- CHAPTER 1 ---
CHAPULINERAS
The Women Who Sell Grasshoppers

The truth is that this is what I do. It is everything. . . .
Chapulines . . . I do not have time to negotiate my life; this is my
life. Even when I am taking care of my children, chapulines are it.
—SEÑORA CARLA MARTÍNEZ, MERCADO BENITO
JUÁREZ, 2023

This chapter introduces the chapulineras I worked with throughout this project. My first round of fieldwork took place in 2006–2007, with a preliminary exploration of the place chapulines hold in the rural Oaxacan diet and everyday eating (Cohen et al. 2009). The project grew in later field seasons to focus on understanding the social milieu in which the chapulineras find themselves. Chapulines have been in the market and on the table for ages; nevertheless, in recent years, the market has developed to include new kinds of eaters, incorporate new kinds of foods, and reflect shifting technologies. Understanding the history of chapulines and the ways that chapulineras have responded to new patterns of production and consumption is critical.

Chapulines are not a pre-Columbian food that remains fundamentally unchanged in the present. The arrival of Spanish colonizers and their foodways following the conquest—as well as the Mexican Revolution, shifts in demand, environmental disasters, violence, social inequalities, and the growth of tourism in the latter half of the twentieth century—affected their meaning, use, and value. These various factors stand as forces to which chapulineras must continually respond today.

Chapulineras live full lives and earn well as they engage with clients in the marketplace. They also live precarious lives and must be ready for the impact of unforeseen crises at a moment's notice. Rural poverty is the backdrop or foundation to much of what they do, but that does not mean that chapulineras are focused on their precarity. Rather, they are actively creating opportunities for success. They work hard. They are in the marketplace and on their phones daily, putting in the hours that are necessary to succeed. Their efforts are rewarded, as they are able to transform their homes and modernize their kitchens and bathrooms, earn the funds to invest in making their children's lives better, and effectively manage the everyday challenges, including accessing health care, that confront them.

Chapulineras know how to sell chapulines. They have spent years working alongside others, often their mothers or grandmothers, and they put in the time necessary to make the job of selling toasted grasshoppers look easy and natural. Their commitment is clear in their marketplace successes, the many clients they manage, and the independence they bring to their work. Their successes are evident in their steady earnings and the clear sense of value they associate with their efforts.

While chapulineras will bargain with their clients, they will leave negotiations if a reasonable price cannot be found. Their efforts and successes are all the more exceptional, given the reality that faces most rural and Indigenous women working in a nation and marketplaces that undervalue their labor and underestimate their abilities (Howell 1999; King 2020; Lyon et al. 2017; Worthen 2015).[1]

Becoming a chapulinera is an effective pathway to prosperity (figure 1.1). It is also a pathway riddled with challenges. Among the challenges that confront chapulineras are biases related to their gender, rurality, social class, limited education, and, in at least some cases, Indigeneity. Chapulineras focus on selling their product and earning money; everything else is secondary. Their focus on selling in the marketplace can make them appear selfish and disinterested in the civic life of their community. In fact, their successes and emphasis on doing well might be assumed to come at a cost to their families and communities. Yet their efforts not only amplify their status as effective businesspeople but also drive economic growth, as their earnings are reinvested in their communities (see also Smyth 2022, 2024). In effect, chapulineras make decisions that reflect self-interested goals while, in the process, balancing the costs

FIGURE 1.1. *Chapulinera, Centro de Abastos, Oaxaca.* Photo by author.

and opportunities of everyday life in response to poverty, precarity, and social inequality (Yamagishi et al. 2014).

Beyond the biases noted, chapulineras do not have the opportunity to freely choose another kind of work. The lack of access to education or job training, gender expectations, and a limited labor market restrict opportunity and the knowledge of what might even be possible (Canedo 2019). Finally, while the state has created programs designed to support and promote the work of rural and Indigenous Oaxacan women, these programs can be problematic, as they assume that the lives of chapulineras are rooted in isolation and Indigeneity. The reality for most chapulineras is a racialized and gendered economic system that denies them choice and implicitly encourages them to act in self-interested ways (Atal et al. 2009; Samson 1995).

The challenges that face chapulineras are physical and intellectual. About 15 percent of the chapulineras we interviewed were dealing with unanticipated, ongoing health-care expenses that put added pressure on them and their incomes. Family members expected the chapulineras in their homes to cover the costs of their consultations, medications, and transportation. This was particularly true during the COVID-19 pandemic. Chapulineras were often expected to support family members, cover the costs of personal protective equipment, and manage household budgets, even as they were asked to support relatives coping with diabetes, hypertension, asthma, depression, or obesity (see Pinzón-Pérez and Santos 2021; Salinas et al. 2010).

One indication of the effectiveness of the chapulineras' response to the health challenges they face at home is that the percentage of individuals facing diabetes or hypertension is lower among their families than the state and Mexican averages. Educational outcomes are also substantially higher for the children of chapulineras, with most children attending *secundaria* (junior high school) and older children earning advanced degrees and attending college, something almost unheard of in rural homes. Nevertheless, the burden placed on chapulineras and the expectations that surround them and their incomes are clear in the pressure that they place on themselves as they juggle multiple responsibilities.

One question that regularly emerged in planning for this work was why chapulineras did not turn to the state, NGOs, or promoters in order to embrace entrepreneurial opportunities in the marketplace. While outside support can be effective, it was not welcomed or trusted, and no one reported engaging outsiders in our interviews. Indigenous women did not seek out available programs, while non-Indigenous rural women avoided any entanglements with state or federal programs or international NGOs.

Chapulineras shared two additional reasons for their disinterest in outsiders who promise economic growth in the future. First, they are not interested in the costs that expanding their efforts might entail; and second, they are already making very good money and are very busy. When we asked one respondent to elaborate on why she refuses to entertain outside support in her business, she started with a one-word answer, "Why?," and went on to argue that there was no reason to work harder.

Chapulines are one food choice among many to consider when eating. Many different edible insects and edible insect by-products are available in Mexico. Historically, insects and insect by-products filled the pre-Columbian menu. Nevertheless, while Mexicans across the nation continue to eat insects, the choices they are making are not the same as those that were made in the past. The practice of entomophagy changed with the conquest, as did the use, value, and meaning of specific kinds of edible insects. And even though production remains largely based in the family and includes feeding the household first, it is mediated by the presence of other foods (including ready-made options) and new forms of consumption.

The introduction of non-native animals and crops by Spanish colonists brought a series of foods and preferences to the region that fundamentally changed eating (Butzer 1988; Gregorio 2021; Robles García 2024). The Spanish also introduced a new worldview and, with it, a vision of the region's peoples (and their foodways) as unequal and consigned to a limited and even negative role in the growth of the Spanish colony and later Mexico (Bérubé and Forde 2024; King and Morell-Hart 2024; Levine and Puseman 2024). The shift in available foods introduced a system of status and demands that defined access and availability according to a hierarchy that rejected Indigenous worldviews and eating habits and popularized the consumption of beef (Butzer 1988).

One of the earliest historical references to chapulines appears in Bernardino de Sahagún's 1577 *Historia general de las cosas de Nueva España* (General history of the things of New Spain). In addition to noting the importance of insects and insect by-products to the Aztec people, he writes that grasshoppers were a critical and welcomed food in season. Nevertheless, Spanish colonists generally ignored local foods as they introduced heretofore unknown crops, animals, and ways of eating (Earle 2010).

The introduction of new foods and ways of eating affected the production and use of commonly accessible and regularly consumed foods (Pérez Rodríguez et al. 2024). With new options, the choice of native, local foods was not as clear. Production also changed as farmers shifted how they worked and how they used their fields to support new crops and create feed for the previously unknown animals (Soleri et al. 2008). These newly available foods provided options that were not necessarily easy for local communities to access, afford, or consume. Not everyone was eating the same foods, and the pressures on production to meet the wishes of the new colonial powers were part of a system that drove increasing inequality between colonizer and colonized (Castañeda Garza

2024). This systemic inequality, codified as the *casta system*—racially based classifications that ranked and organized people according to what Rebecca Earle (2016) describes as "desire and narrative"—continues to affect how Indigenous and rural Oaxacans are regarded and treated into the present (see also Baldomero Quintana et al. 2023).

Many of the foods introduced by the Spanish did not integrate easily into an Indigenous system that had no parallels for grains or livestock. The situation was worsened by Spaniards who doubted the very humanity of the local population. The food that was promoted, planted, and processed was often unavailable to the locals, who could not access seeds or harvests for themselves. Furthermore, complicating the arrival of new foods and crops were blights, droughts, and flooding, which limited growth and decimated livestock (Ficek 2019). These events, as well as demands on local populations to work first for colonists before turning to their own concerns, complicated the access to and availability of foods.

For local peoples in places like rural Oaxaca, decisions on what to eat had become focused on meeting the immediate need of nourishment and managing labor that was demanded by the Spanish. The pressures were all-consuming, particularly during climate events that disrupted daily life (Endfield et al. 2004). Local food production could be threatened, and crops might fail. This was particularly true for the crops and the animals introduced from Spain, which were not well adapted to local conditions (Berdan 1993; Endfield 2012). During the many ecological disasters reported from the seventeenth to the nineteenth centuries and documented by Georgina Endfield and colleagues (2004), chapulines and other Indigenous crops grew more critical to survival. No longer a choice, chapulines and other native crops were a necessity. Nevertheless, in these critical moments, native foods were stigmatized by the colonizers.

Throughout the twentieth century, and particularly during the Mexican Revolution, chapulines, other edible insects, and insect by-products were critical sources of nourishment for rural Oaxacans as they coped with environmental disasters and violence. Working in Santa Ana del Valle in the early 1990s, older villagers recounted how fields were burned and how they abandoned them and found refuge in the mountains to avoid being trapped in conflicts between opposing forces during the Mexican Revolution. Chapulines were a critical food during that period and served as a key protein source for locals who could not tend to their fields or herds (Cohen 1999).

Following the revolution, the Mexican state continued to push Indigenous and rural peoples to leave behind tortillas and adopt a new diet based on bread and other Western foods (Ochoa 2000). In the process, "traditional" foods, including edible insects and insect by-products, were further disparaged. Enrique Ochoa (2000) notes that the state promoted Western foods and styles of eating not only as a healthier alternative but as a nutritional imperative that would usher in eating for a smarter future. In the process, this plan explicitly mocked and criticized native foodways and limited any discussion of the benefits that locally sourced, Indigenous food habits might hold (Otero 2018).

Mexico's Secretaría de Agricultura y Desarrollo Rural (SADER) classifies grasshoppers as a plague animal and potential threat to food crops, a designation that continues to complicate the production of edible insects for human consumption.[2] SADER's negative stance toward chapulines influences and informs public attitudes: In what can only be described as a depressing twist, the disgust and phobic reactions that many people have toward the native consumption of chapulines and other insects became the basis of a joke that came up in several conversations I had with folks who were distancing themselves from rural and Indigenous Oaxacans. Alone and away from others, they would suggest that hiring a couple of Oaxacans was an economical, pesticide-free way of controlling insects (on pest control, see Barrientos-Lozano and Almaguer-Sierra 2006; Dakhel et al. 2020).

The changing history of consumption, the complicated role that insects play in contemporary Mexican agriculture, and the ways in which chapulines are interpreted and used symbolically by locals, visitors, and outsiders remain foundational to this study and were at the center of data collection.

In the first rounds of fieldwork (2006–2008), I focused my efforts on Zimatlán de Álvarez, a town known for its chapulineras. I developed a convenience sample that included five bilingual women who spoke both Spanish and Zapotec and identified as Indigenous, as well as two non-Indigenous women who spoke only Spanish but had grown up in the community and described their grandparents as Indigenous.

In 2022, I revised my efforts and focused my fieldwork in markets and with vendors from different communities and backgrounds.[3] My goal was to identify chapulineras through the marketplace and follow them to their home villages. This approach diversified my sample and allowed me to meet chapulineras from different backgrounds and communities. In my new sample, non-Indigenous women were in the majority, and I was able to capture how their efforts played into the local economy, reproduced structural and social inequalities, and opened opportunities.

Building a snowball sample and following connections from one vendor to another, I successfully identified sixty-three women to complete a survey on their lives, families, and work histories. Of that total, fifty-eight chapulineras identified their hometowns (seventeen in total) as well as where they sold chapulines (see table 1.1).

The majority of the women (just under 67 percent) were from communities south of the state's capital. This is a region of the state that is well known for its chapulines. Of the chapulineras who called southern valley villages home, fourteen were from Santa Lucía Ocotlán, seven were from Zimatlán, and six were from Ocotlán de Morelos. Additionally, four chapulineras who identified as Zapotec were from Santa Inés Yatzeche, a socially and economically marginal community with a high rate of out-migration (see Cohen and Rodriguez 2005). Other towns that appeared in our survey were Ayoquezco de Aldama, San Isidro, Cuilapan de Guerrero, Santa María Vigallo, San Martín Tilcajete, and Zaachila, each home to one or two chapulineras.

Chapulineras from the central valleys clustered around Oaxaca City and represented 12 percent of the total, including six women who lived in the city proper. Two of these women were married and had relocated to Oaxaca City from their natal homes in Puebla and in the Sierra Mixe.[4] One additional chapulinera was from Santa Cruz Xoxocatlán, an independent community that has become an exurb of Oaxaca City. Another chapulinera from the Sierra Mixe traveled regularly to Oaxaca City, where she sells directly to clients in the Tianguis (open-air market) de la Colonia Reforma. Colonia Reforma is a middle-class neighborhood north of the city's center. While she completed our survey, she did not identify her hometown.

Additionally, 16 percent of our sample came from the eastern or Tlacolula branch of the valley. We met and interviewed two chapulineras from Tlacolula, three chapulineras from San Juan Teitipac, and four chapulineras from San Jerónimo Tlacochahuaya. We encountered the

Table 1.1. Chapulinera Hometowns, 2022 Field Season

Town	Region	2020 population	Chapulineras in this study
Oaxaca	Centro	736,000[a]	6
Santa Cruz Xoxocotlán	Centro	100,402	1
San Juan Teitipac	Tlacolula-East	2,668	3
San Jerónimo Tlacochahuaya	Tlacolula-East	2,431	5
Tlacolula	Tlacolula-East	15,219	2
San Jerónimo Yahuiche	Etla-North	2,387	1
Sierra Mixe	Sierra Norte	96,920[b]	1
San Isidro	Zimatlán-South	480	1
Santa Lucía Ocotlán	Zimatlán-South	4,173	14
Zimatlán de Álvarez	Zimatlán-South	14,226	7
Ocotlán de Morelos	Zimatlán-South	23,751	6
Santa Inés Yatzeche	Zimatlán-South	908	4
Ayoquezco de Aldama	Zimatlán-South	4,874	1
Santa María Vigallo	Zimatlán-South	916	1
San Martín Tilcajete	Zimatlán-South	1,975	1
Cuilapan de Guerrero	Zimatlán-South	21,597	2
Zaachila	Zimatlán-South	16,788	2

[a] *Population estimates for Oaxaca City are from 2023.*
[b] *Population estimates for the Sierra Mixe, which encompasses seventeen* municipios *(administrative divisions), are from 2005.*

fewest chapulineras in the northern or Etla branch of the central valleys, with only one chapulinera, who was from San Jerónimo Yahuiche.

The chapulineras we engaged during our 2022 field season ranged from nineteen to eighty-three years of age and averaged forty-seven years of age: 63 percent were between the ages of thirty-three and sixty-one, 19 percent were thirty-two or younger, 17 percent were between the ages of sixty-two and seventy-five, and 2 percent were seventy-six or older. Most of the chapulineras began working in their early twenties, and they often learned how to manage their businesses from their mothers (37 percent) or grandmothers (8 percent). Just over one-third (34 percent) were self-taught and were the first members of their families to sell chapulines. We learned that there were also women who walked away from the marketplace or focused only on their own needs, never joining in the production and sales of chapulines to clients.

The majority of women in our sample (42 percent) were married, though not all had a formal, church wedding. Another 14 percent were living in civil unions, 34 percent were single, 5 percent were widows, and one woman was divorced.

Most of the women we talked to belonged to larger households and had family members to support; nevertheless, chapulineras are independent businesswomen who do not work in tandem with others. While they might consult others around work, labor, and the marketplace, a majority (88 percent) reported making their decisions independently. Additionally, their independence increases as they mature into their roles as businesswomen, with women over fifty-nine years of age managing to work with little to no support from their partners, children, or other family members.

The independence that chapulineras demonstrate does not mean that they are free of responsibilities to others, and most respondents reported supporting at least one child (78 percent). Over half of the women under thirty-three years of age were mothers to children under sixteen years old. In 2007, several women described putting their children to work as a way to keep them occupied and out of trouble. Chapulineras generally work alone, and 80 percent of those interviewed in 2022 harvested on their own, though most hired wageworkers to help collect chapulines. About 20 percent bought raw chapulines directly from other producers. While some children worked in the fields with their mothers, most were left home under the care of a relative or older sibling, who made sure they were fed and, if warranted, got them ready for the school day. Older children were left on their own while their mothers traveled to harvest (and to sell), but with clear instructions for the day. And in the cases where grown children remained at home, they were tasked not with supporting the harvest but with continuing their educations or finding their own work and careers. In one case, a daughter had begun working with her mom only to develop her own clientele and had branched off to work independently.

Chapulineras talked about the value of education throughout our interviews. Chapulineras with young children at home hoped that they would complete compulsory education and have the opportunity to train in technical programs or at a local university. For most chapulineras, their hopes for schooling were a reaction to their own limited classroom experiences. Overall, about 64 percent of the chapulineras we interviewed had completed six years of *primaria* (elementary school), 20 percent had completed *secundaria*, and 5 percent had pursued advanced degrees.[5]

Health care is a concern for everyone. Even though the rates of chronic disease and other health challenges (obesity and hypertension) among the women we met were lower than the state or national averages, 15 percent of the chapulineras we interviewed in 2022 were dealing with both planned and unanticipated health-care expenses that included medications for diabetes, asthma, and hypertension, as well as the costs of managing obesity and mental health counseling.[6] Managing the challenges of the pandemic and fallout from COVID-19, which closed schools and sealed many rural towns, was an unanticipated expense that many women noted put pressure on them. Many chapulineras found that they were caught between managing their business and dealing with markets and schools that were closed from March 2020 through August 2021.

The market for chapulines is large, with tons of grasshoppers moving annually from vendors to consumers in Oaxaca and elsewhere. Many chapulineras export to clients in the United States and will work with import-export shops to reach expat communities abroad (Grieshop 2007). Señora Martínez described sales at home and abroad, noting, "I have my people here. I have my people in Argentina. . . . I have my clients. They call whether now or for the holidays and we get along. Yes, I have thirty years in this market with grasshoppers, in this business. From my grandparents to my family today."

While the total number of kilograms sold year to year and over time in Oaxaca is not available, René Cerritos-Flores and colleagues (2015) estimate that 350,000 tons of chapulines are living on Mexican crops and available for production, with a potential income of USD 350 million (for global patterns of production, see Guiné et al. 2021; van Huis et al. 2013). The vast majority of the chapulineras we interviewed (over 90 percent) reported moving an average of 7.3 kilograms (just over 16 pounds) of chapulines daily. Their sales take many forms. About 90 percent are direct and made to regular customers or clients who have standing orders. Of much less importance and value are irregular sales to outsiders who are wandering the marketplace. Chapulineras describe sales to regular clientele as critical to their survival, while sales to tourists are an unanticipated but welcome "bonus." Chapulineras do not dismiss tourists and outsiders, but they know that these sales will not take the place of regular sales: "There are more tourists, but they're a little bit different. They'll try some grasshoppers, peanuts, *chicatanas*. I say, 'try it, *güero* [lit. "blond," often used to describe a foreigner]. It has chile.' But they are on vacation, so right now there are more, but they'll leave" (Doña Carmen Mendoza, Mercado Benito Juárez, May 2023).

It is typical to encounter young women walking through the marketplace with baskets full of chapulines, selling to anyone who might wander by. These women are usually not full-time chapulineras, and they are not involved in the harvest or preparation of the grasshoppers (activities that consume the entrepreneurs are discussed in chapter 5). These women are casual day laborers who are often hired on the spot and paid something close to the minimum wage.[7] They lack expertise and typically know very little about chapulines, their provenience, or what to do with them. Three of the chapulineras we interviewed (5 percent) had spent time selling for others in return for a set day's wage. Other vendors (8 percent) sold only to other chapulineras or to restauranteurs (not tourists), who would place large, regular orders. Three chapulineras regularly exported chapulines to buyers in the United States and elsewhere abroad. While chapulines are the core product for sale in most market stalls, many chapulineras also sell the seasoning blend *sal de gusano* (59 percent), other vegetables (12 percent), and other seasonal or specialty items (49 percent), including *chicatanas*.

Overall, the experiences of the fifty-eight chapulineras interviewed over the 2022 field season were quite similar. The few differences among the group were attributable to age, education, or marital status. With a few exceptions, Indigeneity fell out as a marker of difference in the experiences of the chapulineras. Indigenous chapulineras (about 7 percent of the chapulineras surveyed in 2022 identified themselves as Indigenous) were younger than their non-Indigenous counterparts, averaging twenty-two years of age versus the forty-seven years of age for non-Indigenous chapulineras. Fewer Indigenous chapulineras owned their land (44 percent), and, while they sold to local consumers, they generally moved less product daily, depending on the sale of chapulines to cover household expenses (33 percent of Indigenous chapulineras versus 22 percent of non-Indigenous chapulineras), and approached their work as a way to put food on the table, rather than a pathway to home improvements and a more independent future. Finally, Indigenous chapulineras sold more chapulines in small batches directly to others within their communities than did non-Indigenous vendors. This likely reflects the rural poverty that confronts Indigenous women in general and that increasingly undermines food sovereignty in Indigenous Oaxacan communities (Martínez-Martínez et al. 2023; Novotny et al. 2021).

Oaxaca is one of Mexico's poorest states (Martínez-Martínez and Rodríguez-Brito 2020). The overwhelming majority of the state's population—and, in particular, the Indigenous and the rural, non-Indigenous populations of the state—must cope with schools that regularly underperform, overcrowded homes that often lack services and amenities, limited health-care choices, and a labor market that consistently disappoints, pays low wages, and has little space for promotion or on-the-job training opportunities (Mason and Beard 2008). In 2020, the Consejo Nacional de Población (CONAPO, National Population Council for Mexico) estimated that 91.5 percent of the state's population was precarious, meaning that they had little to no job security and that opportunities for work (as well as for a living wage) were lacking. Of that total, 43.1 percent of the population was living in moderate poverty, while 23.3 percent was living in extreme poverty.[8]

Moderate to extreme poverty can trap any Oaxacan, yet Indigenous and rural citizens are more likely than their non-Indigenous, urban neighbors to find themselves marginalized and insecure in their daily lives (Núñez-Rocha et al. 2021). This is a severe problem for Oaxaca, where more than 70 percent of the population is identified by the state as Indigenous. Writing on the challenges facing Indigenous communities around the nation, Ana Canedo (2019) estimates that 70 percent of all Indigenous peoples in Mexico live in poverty. In fact, she notes that Indigenous Mexicans are more than twice as likely to live in poverty as their non-Indigenous neighbors. Nevertheless, the gap in income, access to education, and opportunity includes rural, non-Indigenous communities as well. In other words, Indigenous and non-Indigenous rural poor, while distinct from each other in their experiences of marginality and precarity, face a poverty gap that leaves them both at a disadvantage. Poverty, and the fear of slipping into poverty, is a regular, everyday challenge for the majority of women we interviewed and the communities we visited, and with few exceptions, everyone planned their days in response to economic uncertainty and marginality.

Marginality in Mexico is indexed through a combination of nine measures that are taken from census reports published by the Instituto Nacional de Estadística y Geografía (INEGI, National Institute of Statistics and Geography). These nine measures are illiteracy, lack of access to education, lack of access to drainage and modern plumbing, lack of electricity, lack of piped water, the presence of dirt floors, limited privacy (a high number of people in a bedroom), small community population size (fewer than five thousand inhabitants), and percentage of the population with incomes lower than twice the minimum wage (CONAPO 2023). Table 1.2 captures the measure of marginality for the communities that are home to the chapulineras we interviewed and surveyed. The measure is a proxy for economic status and is useful in the discussion of rural poverty in Mexico, as well as serving as an indicator of the inequalities that define life for chapulineras, among others. That said, the measure of marginality does have its limitations. For example, the index ignores gender and does not capture how gender inequalities, including access to political voice in rural communities, can further marginalize a person and limit their access to educational resources, wages, health care, and work opportunities (Puyana Mutis and Márquez Moranchel 2021; Servan-Mori et al. 2014). The index also neglects to account for the impact of Indigeneity or the presence of non-Spanish languages in communities. While non-Spanish languages are tracked by INEGI, the marginality index does not acknowledge how language discrimination confronts native speakers and further limits access. Finally, the index does not refer to the ways in which limits and restrictions amplify acculturative stress, depression, and post-traumatic stress disorder (Olko et al. 2023).

In light of the challenges faced by most Oaxacans, it should not be a surprise that chapulineras—including chapulineras who hail from Indigenous communities—are making decisions that are rooted in the hopes of managing marginality and accessing opportunities (regardless of how limited they might be), rather than opening new avenues for entrepreneurial activity and economic growth (Amorós et al. 2021). In other words, the decisions that chapulineras make are organized to manage the challenges of everyday poverty, maximize limited opportunities, and, most importantly, create spaces for their children's future

Table 1.2. Marginality Scale, 2020

Town	Marginality
Oaxaca de Juárez	very low
Santa Cruz Xoxocotlán	very low
Tlacolula de Matamoros	low
San Jerónimo Yahuiche	low
San Martín Tilcajete	low
San Jerónimo Tlacochahuaya	medium
Zimatlán de Álvarez	medium
Ocotlán de Morelos	medium
Santa María Vigallo	medium
Zaachila	medium
San Juan Teitipac	high
Sierra Mixe	high
San Isidro	high
Santa Lucía Ocotlán	high
Ayoquezco de Aldama	high
Cuilapan de Guerrero	high
Santa Inés Yatzeche	very high

Source: *CONAPO 2023.*

success. Through their efforts, they sow the seeds for their children to have more choice in their lives, better educations, and more opportunities to achieve.

The poverty that defines an Indigenous community and its people is not unique. Rather, it is shared with non-Indigenous poor and marginal rural communities, even if some aspects of poverty are particularly linked to the experiences of Indigenous peoples and create challenges for Indigenous chapulineras (see also Young et al. 1979). Poverty does not discriminate; it is shared across rural Oaxaca and beyond. The poverty that the non-Indigenous, rural poor face is no less disruptive or difficult to escape.

The challenges that confront chapulineras are not rooted in a rural, Indigenous zeitgeist, or in the isolation of their communities. Neither are they limited by decision-making that must inherently correspond to expectations of long-lost traditions. The differences separating Indigenous and rural communities from non-Indigenous, urban centers are rooted in limited educational systems, a lack of economic opportunities, and local expectations that are tempered by generations of discrimination and abuse (Canedo 2019).

First, while educational outcomes are limited for all Oaxacans, Indigenous and rural Oaxacans are more likely to lack schooling than their non-Indigenous counterparts. The average time spent in school for most rural, Indigenous Oaxacans is between five and six years, and bilingual education for students whose second language is Spanish is lacking. Second, while precarity is a challenge for all Oaxacans, Indigenous and rural Oaxacans have fewer opportunities to work and to earn incomes that might mitigate some uncertainty. Third, in a system that is defined by extreme gender-based biases, rural, Indigenous women in Oaxaca suffer. The challenges they face include language barriers that limit the ability of non-native Spanish speakers to engage with the larger market system, partner and domestic violence as well as femicide and exploitation, and discrimination that has accumulated over centuries of bias. Discrimination and abuse make it difficult for all women to achieve, particularly Indigenous rural women, who are taught to expect the worst, regardless of any promises made (see also Briseño-Maas and Bautista-Martínez 2016; Martin and Carvajal 2016). For most Indigenous, rural Oaxacans, there is no expectation that things will get better. Yet chapulineras go into their work with a mindset focused on doing the best they can.

The continued challenges that confront chapulineras contrast with federal statistics, which note a decline in overall poverty in Oaxaca since 2016. In fact, marginality in rural and Indigenous Oaxacan communities remains quite high and surged during the COVID-19 pandemic (Cohen and Mata-Sánchez 2021; Ibarra-Nava et al. 2020). The challenges are real, and while the Mexican economy is in recovery, they continue to confront chapulineras daily. Their success should be highlighted, given the many difficulties they face; nevertheless, uncertainty prevails, there is little leeway for unanticipated emergencies, and most women commented on the increasing stress of daily life in the region.

Chapulineras are under no illusion that aid is forthcoming. Rather, they have developed the tools necessary to cope with the marginality of their hometowns and precarities that they confront daily. While it is clear that community matters to these women, chapulineras are "poised in a web of potentiality conducive to appropriate courses of conduct afforded by interconnection with other entities in their environment" (Warde 2016, 51). In other words, they hope that the future will be brighter than the past, and they stand a better chance of succeeding if they put in the effort while clearly understanding that there is no support system backing them up if they fail.

── CHAPTER 2 ──
THE HARVEST AND PRODUCTION

I learned with my grandparents . . . my grandparents, my parents, and others while I was growing up. I learned to target the chapulines and grab the big ones. You grab the big ones with your hands, scoop the little ones with a net. . . . From there you've got it.
—DOÑA CARMEN MENDOZA, MERCADO BENITO JUÁREZ, OAXACA, 2022

I began with my husband's family, following their traditions after we married. My husband would bring me chapulines in large quantities, and with him and my in-laws' support, I started to cook and sell. It wasn't easy at first, and I did hesitate some, but I liked the money I made. Those first times, I sold everything, and now I have been selling chapulines for twenty-three years.
—DOÑA TERESA SILVA, TLACOLULA, 2008

Doñas Carmen Mendoza and Teresa Silva describe the harvest as a tradition that is learned from family. It is not complicated: While chapulineras have innovated around the changing market, shipping to expats living outside the region and adapting to crises like the pandemic, the harvest continues to follow a regular pattern. Learning to harvest happens in the moment, with family and friends in the cool of the morning, just as the sun rises. It is work that demands good hand-eye coordination and that can be exhausting as harvesters move up and down rows of *maíz* and alfalfa, but it is not hard. For women who have young children, letting them run with nets to catch chapulines in the early morning is a good way to start the day. When a gringo joins in the harvest, the day becomes a fun diversion.

I learned how to harvest chapulines in 2007, with the help of Señora Miranda Reyes, a restaurant owner and chef who had turned her roadside café near the town of Mitla in the eastern branch of the central valleys into a destination for tour buses (figure 2.1). During a visit to her home, I asked whether she would teach me how to harvest chapulines, and whether I could follow along to document and photograph the process. She agreed and told me to arrive at her home early the next morning, around four o'clock, to join her for the harvest. I demurred and suggested that maybe we could push the time back, as I needed daylight to photograph and document the event. Laughing, Señora Reyes and two of her older children just shook their heads and lectured me: "You cannot harvest after the sun is up and it starts to get hot." She continued, "The chapulines will jump away in the warmth of the sun. In the early morning, when it is cooler and as the sun is rising, they are slow and easy to scoop up."

We came to a compromise. We would not conduct a proper early morning harvest. Instead, in the light of day, they would teach me how to harvest. I would join them, and I could take as many photographs as I liked.

The next day, I arrived, camera and notebook in hand. The family was set with a few nets and a couple of mesh bags. Together, we walked to the edge of her milpa, where there were plenty of chapulines sunning themselves on corn stalks. With a serious look, Señora Reyes reminded me of the rules—harvest early and be quick. I was making a mockery of how things should work. No one with sense would set off to harvest chapulines midday. Yet here we were, all in service to ethnographic documentation.

How often is a gringo in the field, taking pictures of the harvest? Not very often, it turned out. Everyone found the process entertaining. Between their laughter and jokes at my expense, the harvest was nominally successful. Not only did I have a chance to take photographs, I also learned how to gather chapulines, dashing about with my plastic bag. The experience ended with a handful of chapulines ready for toasting. I did not catch a lot, and while my efforts did not amount to much, I had learned. The heat of the midday sun did its work, and we finished the photographs and returned to the kitchen to process our catch.

FIGURE 2.1. *Chapulinera in her restaurant, Mitla, Oaxaca. Photo by author.*

Back in the kitchen, Señora Reyes demonstrated the steps involved in the preparation of chapulines. First, we cleaned our catch, which primarily involved sorting the random insects from the grasshoppers we wanted. Second, we added my catch to a large cardboard box for storage. Finally, we opened a box and began to prepare for toasting. Toasting starts by boiling water, adding a splash of *limón* (lime), and dunking the chapulines. It takes only a few minutes to boil chapulines, and in the process they turn a rich, appetizing red. After their bath, the chapulines are tossed onto a comal to toast with garlic, salt, and chiles. Once they are toasted, there are myriad possibilities, from simple tacos to complicated entrées and sauces.

HARVESTING

The Turkish playwright Mehmet Murat İldan is popularly quoted as writing, "The heaven of a grasshopper is the wheat field; the heaven of man is the same place, the very earth itself where we get our food and build our happiness!" Trade the Anatolian wheat fields for Oaxacan milpas planted with alfalfa and *maíz*, and you have created heaven. Chapulines need nothing more, and chapulineras are ready to build happiness.

Chapulines appear in the central valleys with the arrival of the spring rains. The hatchlings emerge from egg clusters that are deposited on leaf litter or in the ground. Young nymphs emerge as miniature copies of adults and experience a series of molts (an incomplete metamorphosis) as they mature over the course of about a month.

Chapulines can travel quite far as adults; nevertheless, milpas provide a great deal of cover and safety. In fact, the chapulines that live among humans and fill milpas are often described as "semi-domesticated." While a few chapulineras noted a decline in the number of chapulines harvested over time, in general, they are so numerous that there is almost always an abundance to be had (see Yen 2015 on farming insects).

The nymphs, often called *nenes* (babies), develop an ability to fly quickly, and, as they mature, they typically relocate from fields of alfalfa to *maíz* fields. The shift in their home plants and their diet influences their flavor (Poshadri et al. 2018).[1] Nymphs are found predominantly in alfalfa, and the crop lends a flavor that is described as *más dulce* (sweeter) by the local population. Adult chapulines are more likely to settle in *maíz* fields, and their taste is described as *amargo* (bitter).

Preparing chapulines for sale begins with their harvest, and 80 percent of the women we interviewed collect chapulines from their milpas and communal lands that they can access within their home communities. Conversely, those chapulineras who lack land or whose milpa is not producing (about 20 percent of our sample) venture a bit farther from home to access fields and often buy from sellers, sometimes purchasing chapulines that are already toasted. Over time, the relationship between chapulinera and harvester grows stronger, and vendors often return to the same harvesters from one season to another. Harvesters who supply chapulineras are from families that do not engage in sales themselves. These families seem content to deliver chapulines to chapulineras, and while the price paid is minimal, sometimes only a few hundred pesos for many kilograms, the work is regular and manageable.

Of course, there are many ways to modify the harvest. Señora Magdalena Velasco (San Martín, June 2022) noted that while she occasionally harvested on her own—using her milpa and accessing family holdings—she also relied on her neighbors' children as well as her own to collect chapulines for a small fee.

Señora Velasco's approach is typical. She harvested on her own and from her milpa, as did just over half (52 percent) of the women surveyed.

In addition, and as the chapulines in her milpa declined in number as the season progressed, she contracted with other suppliers. Her approach did not always produce enough chapulines to keep up with demand, and she noted that her sales were not as large as those of some other chapulineras working in the region. Gesturing with her hands to mimic a heavy bag, she described her efforts as "small scale, we don't deliver per kilo or kilo after kilo."

Indigenous Zapotec women were less likely to harvest from their own land (42 percent), and they would typically collect chapulines on communal holdings or harvest from the private holdings of extended family and friends. Nevertheless, their approach to preparing chapulines was quite similar to that of their non-Indigenous counterparts, as noted by Sofia Baptista (Santa Lucía, July 2008), who commented, "I get my chapulines in two ways, by going to the milpa [mine and others] or buying them from a lady in Santa Inés who has already toasted them."

The harvest follows the life cycle of the grasshoppers and the calendar. Harvesters begin work in the spring, collecting nymphs as they emerge. Through the summer, harvesters collect on fields of both alfalfa and *maíz*. Nymphs and younger chapulines tend to cluster in alfalfa, moving to *maíz* as they mature. Harvesters follow the grasshoppers, shifting from alfalfa fields to *maíz* accordingly.

The harvest takes place in the early hours of the morning and begins just as the sun is rising. While chapulines can be caught later in the day, as I documented in my experiences with Señora Reyes, waiting for better light means that the grasshoppers warm up, become more active, and are able to quickly jump away from any sudden movement or threat. The cool morning and limited sunlight render the diurnal chapulines less active and easier to catch.

To harvest chapulines, people use butterfly nets, cloth bags, pillowcases, and even disposable plastic bags. Harvesters move up and down the rows of a field, waving their nets and bags in a regular pattern. Contributing to the ease of the harvest is the uniformity of the fields. Regular rows limit surprises, and human intervention in the fields means that there is a lack of other dangerous animals and predators that might consume the grasshoppers. Unfortunately, during the harvest, it is easy to catch a lot of other insects, but there is time to sort them later. During the harvest it is important to keep nets and bags closed and limit any possible escape.

Collectors deposit their chapulines in cardboard boxes for safekeeping. The boxes will serve as a home for the chapulines for the foreseeable future. Carried away once the harvest is completed, the chapulines are sorted by size and unwanted insects are removed. The best way to produce clean chapulines is to place the box in a cool space, where the insects can calm down, become inactive, and pass any wastes. It is important not to rush; opening a box full of agitated chapulines in the sun will most likely give them the opportunity to jump away. Jumping chapulines can move at a rate of ten feet (or three meters) per second. At that speed, it is easy for a grasshopper to spring from an open box and clear the patio of a home.

Once the trapped insects have calmed, it is easy to sort them. The harvester knows what chapulineras want, and non-grasshoppers are thrown aside. Sometimes it is necessary to sort nymphs and adults, but the life cycle of the grasshopper plays out in such a way that most chapulines encountered during any specific time in the harvest are of the same age and size.

Though the harvest is uncomplicated, it does demand experience and skill. Señora María Hernández (San Nicolás, Ocotlán, July 2008) shared that "no one in my family harvests chapulines; rather, I work with *alfalfaros* [alfalfa farmers] who have worked the fields and have the know-how to carefully time the harvest to best catch the chapulines."

While it might seem as if anytime during the season can work for collecting chapulines, harvesters take advantage of the chapulines' life cycle and maturity and plan their efforts accordingly. The age and maturity of the chapulines are also critical to chapulineras, who sell differently sized chapulines at different prices. The difference in price—nymphs are typically more expensive than adults—is crucial as chapulineras prepare many hundreds of kilograms for sale.

The importance of timing is clear in Señora Hernández's preference for young nymphs, which she sells for a premium in the Zimatlán marketplace. Working with *alfalfaros*, she plans when to harvest and knows that there are enough hands to capitalize on the early life cycle of the chapulines in support of higher prices. Other vendors, including Señora Sofía Baptista (Santa Lucía, July 2008), prefer to wait and harvest larger adults. While she works throughout the season, Baptista puts in extra effort as the season draws to a close. With the support of her suppliers, she hoards adult chapulines and brings them to the market through the winter, when she can place an additional premium or markup on her product.

While most of the women we interviewed learned to harvest from their mothers and grandmothers, others apprenticed themselves or were self-taught. There is a tradition of harvesting chapulines with children, and it is an effective way to put energetic kids to work. Indigenous women are more likely than non-Indigenous women to rely on family members during the harvest and in the processing and sale of chapulines.

Non-Indigenous women rely far less heavily on their families for support in the fields and during production. Most successful chapulineras commented that it is a challenge to rouse their children before dawn to participate in the harvest, and few children have the patience and energy to produce chapulines in amounts that can support larger sales. More importantly, and as will become clear in the discussion of the economics of the marketplace, non-Indigenous women are focused on building their business to earn enough to send their children to technical schools and college. Chapulineras do not want to burden their children with the difficulties of the harvest.

Further capturing the importance chapulineras place on the business of chapulines, a small but growing number are buying harvested and prepared chapulines from others, skipping the harvest and preparation process entirely and thereby saving time that they described as better spent on working with clientele. Finally, chapulineras from Puebla and other states have joined local vendors to sell chapulines in the marketplace. There is little engagement between the oaxaqueña and poblana chapulineras. In fact, chapulineras from Oaxaca accuse the women from Puebla of working with farmers who use pesticides to incapacitate the chapulines before collecting them to process and sell. While there is no evidence of this happening, the rumor captures the tensions that surround competition.

Harvests, as noted, take place on a specific schedule and in specific locations, which leads to a uniformity in the size and flavor of the chapulines collected. Uniformity is further ensured during the cleaning process, which eliminates other insects that might have been gathered inadvertently and gives the resting chapulines the opportunity to pass any wastes. Sorting also allows a producer to better know their stock. The harvesters gain a sense of their product, its size and quality, and the volume there is to sell. They learn what they can expect to charge and earn, whether the chapulines are for themselves or for other chapulineras. Knowing the harvest also allows the chapulinera to better plan for specific client requests and to calculate how much extra she might have on hand to sell on the open market, to restauranteurs, and to outsiders.

Once cleaned and sorted, the chapulines are left in their boxes in a cool part of the home to sit undisturbed for one to three days. During this time, and generally for the rest of their captivity, they are not fed. This accomplishes a few things. First and foremost, it gives the chapulines time to void any wastes in their system. Second, waiting to prepare the chapulines keeps them alive and fresh until it is time to cook. This is important. While chapulines can keep over long periods, they can spoil, and spoiled chapulines are unappetizing.

Giving chapulines time to digest and void any wastes has the effect, according to local stories, of "promising a better taste." Many women we interviewed maintained that chapulineras from outside the state do not let their chapulines rest. Instead, they sort and cook chapulines promptly upon harvest to get them to market more quickly. Julián Ramírez, a vendor in Oaxaca's central market and the only chapulinero we encountered (Centro de Abastos, July 2007), contended that large-scale producers use chiles to cover the bad taste of chapulines that have not rested or that have grown stale while waiting to be sold. Commenting on the difference between chapulines from Oaxaca and those from Puebla, he exclaimed, "What am I, a vendor from Puebla? I never put chiles in my chapulines. If they're fresh, you don't need to do that! They should be fresh and unflavored, cooked with a little *sal de gusano* and garlic. These chapulines are not good [gesturing to vendors he did not know], the growers don't rest them, and they have a bad taste because of it!"

While Señor Ramírez was clear in his criticism of vendors from outside the state, we learned that many chapulineras flavor—or, as they describe it, *paint*—their chapulines with chiles before going to market. Furthermore, while chapulineras from Puebla may follow a different schedule for production and not give their harvests as much time to rest (something that is not clear), there is no evidence that the chapulines originating from Puebla harbor dangerous levels of waste before they are prepared (Imathiu 2020; Poma et al. 2017).

COOKING

After the chapulines are clean and rested, it is time for cooking. Cooking chapulines takes skill, and timing is important. Boiled too long, the chapulines are mushy, and without the right ingredients the flavors can be off. Señora Bianca Montes (San Pedro Mártir, Ocotlán, Oaxaca, July 2008) succinctly described the process: "To prepare chapulines, you boil them for five minutes. Then squeeze the water out before tossing them in a *cazuela* [casserole] or on a comal. Add some *limón*, garlic, *sal de gusano*, and chile. Toast them for ten minutes, until they are ready to sell" (see figure 2.2).

The immersion in boiling water is perhaps the most critical step in processing chapulines. Before dunking the chapulines, the cook adds some *limón* and several garlic cloves. The boil dispatches the chapulines and gives them a final rinse before toasting. The inclusion of *limón* and garlic adds flavor. Additionally, the heat of the boiling water begins the release of astaxanthin, a carotenoid pigment also common in crustaceans. The interaction frees the astaxanthin, which binds to crustacyanin (a carotenoprotein like astaxanthin) to turn the chapulines a rich red.

Once boiled, the chapulines are ready to toast. While chapulines can be fried in oil and flavored with chiles, the first toasting is often oil free. Grabbing a handful of prepared chapulines, a chapulinera tosses them onto a hot comal or into a *cazuela* for about ten minutes. Adding more lemon juice, garlic, and *sal de gusano* or regular table salt completes the transformation of chapulines into an appetizing treat.

To develop a more distinctive flavor and crispier texture, chapulines can be toasted at a higher heat and seasoned with a variety of spices and chiles (for a history of chiles in Oaxaca, see García-Gaytán et al. 2017; Manzanero-Medina et al. 2020; Powis et al. 2013). A cast-iron pan in place of a comal will also impart a different flavor, as will a shorter boil balanced against a quick sauté with vegetables in a little oil.

Once toasted, the finished chapulines are heaped into large baskets.

FIGURE 2.2. *Preparation of chapulines. Photo by Francisco Montiel-Ishino.*

The baskets allow air to circulate through the mounds of chapulines. Many chapulineras also use plastic bags to hold the toasted critters, but using bags risks locking in moisture that can promote spoilage and leave the chapulines soggy.

EATING

Eating chapulines is a complex sensory experience marked by a combination of aroma, appearance, expectations, flavors, personal taste, and traditions (Locher et al. 2005; Patil and Young 2012). The aroma combines *limón*, garlic, *sal de gusano*, and chile, filling the nose. The red of the toasted chapulines captures the eyes. The seasonal wait to consume builds anticipation, while the flavors carry a history of eating that triggers a sense of desire that can only be answered through consumption (Boesveldt and Parma 2021). The mounds of freshly toasted chapulines, filling basket after basket, invite the consumer to dig in and partake of a never-empty plate. Oaxacans celebrate the season and the arrival of chapulines with great anticipation. The intensity is both cultural and biological, but it is not driven by hunger. It is anticipatory and celebratory, driven by recall, psychology, and repetition (Spence 2021). Chapulines are critical to everyday life, worldview, and conduct (Warde 2016).

Chapulines are like Proust's madeleines, reminding the eater of childhood. In years past, rural Oaxacans ate chapulines amid climate crises (drought and earthquakes), violence around the Mexican Revolution, and crop failures, as well as when other proteins were unavailable. They also ate them outside of crises; chapulines were simply always on the menu. Today, in a way that recalls those crises as moments of resilience, and traditions as practices that bring heritage home, chapulines are welcomed. Through their regular presence on the table, they become a reminder of the power local foods hold.

There are many ways to prepare chapulines. Some folks serve them as a main dish. They are particularly popular in tacos: Chapulines are heavily sprinkled on tortillas, warmed and fresh from the comal, and then topped with salsa and *limón*, making a delicious, quick meal. Other chefs and cooks maintain that chapulines are best as a side dish. Doña Teresa Silva shared how to make a quick and tasty salsa, a perfect topping for almost anything: "Prepare your chapulines and boil [them] with your tomatillos. Sauté garlic and onions in a little oil and then combine these ingredients in a blender with some water, adding *limón* and *sal de gusano*." Chapulines can also be an ingredient in a more complicated recipe. Doña Carmen Mendoza shared her recipe for a special mole made with chapulines (Mercado Benito Juárez, May 2023): "Clean and prepare a kilo of chapulines for eating. Roast them with some additional salt and then grind [them] into a paste with your other ingredients: oregano, onions, cacao, cinnamon, raisins, fried bananas, crisp cookies, and about half a kilo of guajillo and ancho chiles. Cook and divide a chicken and serve with rice and tortillas."

Upscale restauranteurs and chefs innovate with chapulines, and urbane Oaxacans argue that it is an unimaginative waste to simply roll them into a tortilla. Reimagining chapulines as a fusion of Oaxaca's Indigenous past and its global future, restauranteurs, chefs, foodies, and outsiders use edible insects in new and trendy combinations.[2]

The contrast between these groups and locals creates a tension that divides them along sociocultural lines. Locals know chapulines as an important food first, and they do not hide the insects' value as a coveted protein that has been welcomed for ages. Outsiders, on the other hand, are critical of local consumers and associate their consumption of chapulines with rural poverty and Indigeneity. Nonlocals view the consumption of chapulines as a tradition that has been lost in time, as something representative of the rural poor and Indigenous populations' failure to adapt to new ways of eating and existing. The differences in use and consumption reflect the inequalities that separate rural and Indigenous populations from their urban and urbane counterparts.[3]

No one eats chapulines because they must or in response to a biological or cultural imperative. Eating chapulines is about choice, and choices have changed through time and as Oaxaca has grown as a destination for tourists, foodies, and others (Sammells 2019). Rural Oaxacans make choices that are influenced by factors that city dwellers often ignore. Foodies and tourists visiting the city make different choices. For locals, chapulines are one of the regular foods that they look forward to eating. For outsiders, chapulines reflect the sense of adventure that comes with eating edible insects and ostensibly consuming a version of the past. Yet, regardless of their motivations, anyone can decide to eat chapulines. Their choice in this regard reflects a conjuncture of experiences, ease of access, availability and cost, need, traditions, expectations, and history.

The factors that influence decision-making also influence taste, or at least the perception of taste (Suzuki et al. 2021). Therefore, it is critical to recognize that even as people eat the same chapulines whether they are locals or outsiders, they may not taste the same things. In rural Oaxaca and for Indigenous Oaxacans, chapulines are abundant and cheap; they are delicious, ubiquitous, and common in local kitchens (figure 2.3). People are happy to talk about eating chapulines in part because they are a regular part of meals. Chapulines are a seasonal treat that people ask for and enjoy.

For rural and Indigenous Oaxacans, eating chapulines is about more than the tangy crunch of a tortilla filled with freshly prepared grasshoppers; it is about the season, warm weather, and family, and, as described by several of our respondents, it is about eating clean, filling, healthy, and safe food. While rolling chapulines into a fresh tortilla with a little salsa is common, some of the best preparations in rural Oaxaca combine chapulines with vegetables, creating colorful, festive bursts of freshness that celebrate the abundance of valley gardens.

FIGURE 2.3. *Chapulinera, Sunday market, Tlacolula. Photo by author.*

The presence of chapulines in city kitchens and on the menus of fine restaurants does not change the value they hold for rural and Indigenous Oaxacans. In fact, Señora Petrona Morales (Ocotlán, July 2009) commented that her children and grandchildren had no qualms combining tortillas and cold cereals (typically corn flakes) and finishing the day with *caldo* (broth/soup) before going out for a hamburger. The fear that chapulines will become increasingly commodified and potentially priced out of reach for locals or replaced by nontraditional, nonlocal fare (like hamburgers) has not come to pass.

Important throughout the central valleys, chapulines are not an everyday treat for outsiders. For urban Oaxacans, however, chapulines are a ready snack, often found in a bowl on the kitchen table. Restauranteurs, particularly those restauranteurs who focus on serving tourists and foodies visiting the state, present chapulines with mezcal and in innovative ways to promote alcohol sales by fostering dare culture. To encourage alcohol consumption, they wrap chapulines in stories of the past and the state's Indigenous heritage. Yet even as they frame the contemporary consumption of chapulines as a sign of Indigeneity and rural poverty, they emphasize the challenge of insect-eating and "dare" consumption. The dare transforms chapulines, playing up the "ick factor" (Hamerman 2016), rendering the question of whether locals eat them as part of their everyday lives almost beside the point. For visitors to Oaxaca, edible insects are disgusting, and chapulines are imagined as a last resort. The dare challenges the consumer to eat something that is outside the domain of what is considered edible or normal (Serpico et al. 2021).

— PART II —
EATING AND THINKING CHAPULINES

— CHAPTER 3 —
CHAPULINES ON THE TABLE

We usually eat the same foods, even during different seasons. But if it is late July or August, that is when there are fresh chapulines to find.
—DOÑA IVANNA HIPOLITO, ZIMATLÁN, 2008

When there is an event, you want some *botanas* [snacks], like this bag of chapulines. Flavored with garlic and some peanuts, it's just right.
—DOÑA CARLA MARTÍNEZ, MERCADO BENITO JUÁREZ, 2022

Right now, when there are a lot of chapulines, I have to tell my kids not to eat them. They have enough, and we need to sell them! That is hard because the kids want to eat them.
—EUGENIA RODRÍQUEZ, SAN MARTÍN TILCAJETE, 2022

There are many food options available to hungry Oaxacans; chapulines are one (figure 3.1). Sometimes deciding what to eat is straightforward. The consumer chooses foods that are available, plentiful, and easy to prepare. More often, the choice is more complicated and influenced by assumptions of edibility, age and status, knowledge, experience, traditions, and history, as well as timing and meal organization (Peterson and Freidus 2023). Deciding what to eat also reflects a consumer's intellectual and physical needs. In addition, how an individual, as a member of

FIGURE 3.1. Chapulinera, panadería *(bakery)*, Mercado Zimatlán, Zimatlán, Oaxaca. Photo by Andrew Mitchel.

a household, will meet and cover the costs of food, respond to the availability of a particular item, and adapt to the moment, expectations, and experience can influence outcomes.

Just because Oaxacans like chapulines does not mean that they are always a first choice or that in their place another insect will do. Doña Ivanna (Zimatlán, July 2008) shared how important new foods and new preparations can be: "We like to try different foods like *rajas* [sliced peppers]. The peppers are roasted and cut into thin slices, and the seeds are cleaned. Then they are fried in oil with sliced onions. When they are ready, I add some seasoning. Cooked a few minutes and served with more cheese, it is ready to eat."

While many foods compete for space in the daily diet, chapulines are an important seasonal choice for many. In most homes there are bowls filled with chapulines just waiting to be eaten. Chapulines appear in lots of dishes, but they are not often the main course. People opt for chapulines any time, but particularly early in the season, and why not? As Elena López (Ocotlán, July 2008) argued: "There is no reason not to eat chapulines. They are natural . . . and meats, well, you don't know where they are from, and they can carry diseases."

Chapulines wrapped in a tortilla and served as a taco with a little salsa are the perfect bite. And yet, even amid their love for chapulines, most Oaxacans find other insects rather off-putting and inedible, viewing them much like most outsiders raised on a Western, meat-centric, entomophobic diet (Pérez-Lloréns 2024). Take crickets, for example. Although crickets are often called chapulines when they appear as an ingredient in mass-marketed high-protein flour mixes and chocolate energy bars in the United States and online, Oaxacans do not like them. They do not mistake crickets for grasshoppers; crickets are *grillos*, not chapulines. Oaxacans will not eat *grillos*.

Curious about the reasoning that separates a grasshopper from a cricket, we asked people to talk about their choices. For nearly everyone, it came down to taste. Crickets are bitter; grasshoppers are not. And while a range of flavors and seasonings impart unique flavors to chapulines, crickets are always bitter. Several women bemoaned their inability to work with crickets, noting that these insects are cheaper and easier to raise than grasshoppers, as they have a shorter growth cycle, reproduce rapidly, and need little to eat. Nevertheless, chapulines are always only grasshoppers, not bitter crickets (Magara et al. 2020).

Chapulines are a tradition that endures for rural and Indigenous Oaxacans, regardless of their age, social status, or experience. Their value as a tradition continues to affect the choices consumers make when they are prepared and eaten (Gladstone 2023; Hernández Ramírez 2023). While new foods abound and younger Oaxacans ask for dishes their parents and grandparents have never eaten and often don't know, chapulines continue to cross generational lines (Hernández Ramírez et al. 2021).

Packaged and ready-made foods are an important option in homes for quick meals, as well as for older children who serve as caregivers. For several families, including households that have lost members to migration or that are headed by a single parent, the speed and ease with which packaged and ready-made foods can be served is an important way to conserve energy and time. Several informants noted pizza's popularity with their children, but also shared that they consider it to be *comida de la chatarra* (junk food).

Junk food is more than a category of low-nutrition, high-calorie food. It is food that threatens health and well-being (see, e.g., Armendariz et al. 2022; Pérez-Ferrer et al. 2020). Señora Lorena Muñoz (Barrio El Pajarito, Zimatlán, July 2008) shared: "Junk food isn't good . . . like *sabritas* [chips] and *sopa maruchan* [ramen]. I know a woman in Zimatlán who gave her daughter *sopa maruchan* every day, and now [the daughter] has anemia. My own sons eat a lot of pizza when they are busy. They like pizza and hamburgers, but I don't. I don't like canned things." While it is not clear that ramen causes anemia, there is evidence that unfortified pasta noodles can contribute to poor nutrition and iron deficiencies (Le et al. 2007), and these are the foods that children often demand.

The list of favorite foods is not always populated with newly introduced, prepackaged fare. Sometimes the list includes local ingredients or local dishes enhanced with the addition of cheeses and fried. Columba Avendaño (San Lorenzo, July 2008) noted how diverse the list of locally made foods can be as she enumerated the dishes her children requested: "They want a lot of different things: *tasajo frito* [thin, dried beef], *chiles rellenos* [stuffed peppers], *carne frita* [fried pork], *taquitos al pastor* [marinated, thinly sliced pork tacos], *hamburguesas* [hamburgers], pizza."

One way some families diversify their diets and supplement what they eat is through *huertas familiares* (kitchen gardens). *Huertas familiares* are critical to families, creating the opportunity to grow the fruits, herbs, and vegetables that are part of the food landscape and central to Oaxacan cooking traditions (see Everett 2004). In rural Oaxaca, people use their gardens to supplement and complement the milpa and store-bought foods (Arellanes Cancino and Sosa Perdomo 2019; Gómez Sal et al. 2014). A kitchen garden does not need to be large, and in some rural Oaxacan homes, it is no more than a few square meters where herbs and chiles are found. Nevertheless, *huertas familiares* are often home to a diversity of plants and are a critical source of fresh fruits and vegetables.

Much like chapulines, the diverse plants grown in a garden can translate to sales and food security (Aguilar-Støen et al. 2009; Manzanero-Medina et al. 2020). During the COVID-19 pandemic, when most markets were closed—or, if open, often lacking in fresh produce—kitchen gardens became even more important.

Not all families have a *huerta familiar*, however. Columba Avendaño, whom we interviewed in San Lorenzo, noted that she does not cultivate vegetables and that her compound lacks any fruit trees. Instead, she "buys all of her foods at the market." Families that lack access to gardens and a milpa do not necessarily eat less fruit or vegetables, but they pay for foods and purchase their produce from markets. Their reliance on the marketplace can drive food insecurity, as they must budget to cover costs while contending with availability, seasonality, and other expenses (Ibarra et al. 2011).

Most Mexicans, including most Oaxacans, follow clear patterns as they choose what to eat. A review of food research in Mexico notes that over 75 percent of the population regularly consumes *maíz* (mostly in the form of tortillas), beans and squash, tomatoes, chiles, and onions (Valerino-Perea et al. 2019). Tortillas are a central part of every meal. Our informants were quite clear: A meal without tortillas was not complete.

Maíz aside, regions have their own food preferences. Selene Valerino-Perea and colleagues (2019) note that the diet of the northern part of the country includes more rice, as well as flour-based tortillas and breads, while that of central Mexico includes more seafood and some insects, particularly *escamoles, chicatanas*, and *axayacatl* (water bugs). Southern Mexico, including the state of Oaxaca, has the highest rate of entomophagy in the nation (Ramos-Elorduy 2002), and more than 75 percent of studies conducted on foodways in the region note the value of chapulines, *chicatanas*, and insect larvae.[1]

The importance of *maíz* in the diet and its central place throughout the country belie the complex choices that confront Mexicans today, regardless of their status, ethnicity, or marginality. The opening of the marketplace to global foods—along with the growing availability of meat (Estévez-Moreno and Miranda-de la Lama 2022) and ready-made and ultra-processed foods (Marrón-Ponce et al. 2019)—has fundamentally changed the way Mexicans eat.[2] Nevertheless, for many rural and Indigenous Oaxacans, ready-made and ultra-processed foods are costly and out of reach, as explained by Señora Adriana Soledad González (Zimatlán, July 2008): "Throughout the year we usually cook and eat the same thing, although there are some vegetables that are seasonal. During the rainy months we tend to eat more *sopa de guías* [a hardy vegetable soup with squash, squash flowers, *maíz*, and aromatics]. We also eat more chapulines when they are in season."

Señora González's choices reflect seasonal patterns, the emergence of certain plants, and the systemic rural poverty that defines the region and her community. Though she has access to local markets and employment, food options are limited by seasonality and wages. Importantly, wages in Oaxaca continue to lag the national average. Even with regular employment in Oaxaca City's tourist industry, wages remain low, and it can be difficult to cover expenses even with work (Canedo 2019; Ramos et al. 2020).[3] It is no surprise that Señora González struggles to put food on the table, as her earnings are limited and as her labor is undervalued due to these low wages and the informality of her work.

The limits on rural women reflect the structural inequalities that define rural and Indigenous life for many families (Murphy and Selby 1985; Villalobos Portilla 2024). In fact, we asked informants to track their meals over two weeks in 2008. While everyone had enough food, proteins were limited, and menus were repetitive, with a heavy reliance on tortillas and stews (see table 3.1).

Poverty explains the food that is on the table as well as the technology that is available in the rural kitchen. The costs of large kitchen appliances put stoves and refrigerators out of reach for many rural families. The absence of most appliances through time means that refrigerators and stoves are still rather exceptional and simply do not fit into the local mindset. Additionally, electricity throughout the region is plagued by spikes and failures in transmission that wreak havoc on equipment.

Many rural and Indigenous families keep two kitchens to prepare foods in ways that follow long-held practices: An outdoor kitchen with a fire pit is used to prepare tortillas, while an indoor kitchen with a gas stove and pantry is used to prepare other dishes, including soups (see von Bremzen 2023, 187–242). In many other cases, and particularly for Indigenous families that live in extreme poverty, there is no second kitchen, and modern technologies, including gas stoves and refrigerators, are too costly to be present. While the front-end costs of many appliances, like stoves, microwave ovens, and refrigerators, are dropping,

Table 3.1. Typical Meals for Rural Oaxacan Families, 2008

	Desayuno (breakfast)	*Almuerzo* (lunch, second breakfast)	*Comida* (main afternoon meal)	*Cena* (dinner)
Family 1	bread, coffee	beans with salsa, water	rice, beans	leftovers, sometimes just coffee
Family 2	bread, coffee (9 a.m.)	pasta, soup, soda	rice, stew, soda, flavored water (3 p.m.)	leftovers, pan dulce, coffee or soda
Family 3	milk, bread (9:30 a.m.)	pasta, soup with vegetables, water	salsa with eggs, beans, meat, chorizo, water (after school)	none
Family 4	coffee, hot chocolate (8 a.m.)	breakfast foods, beans, rice	beans, rice, eggs, cheese, soda (2–3 p.m.)	leftovers, often just coffee with milk (7 p.m.)
Family 5	children: cereal, bread, coffee adults: milk, coffee, hot chocolate, bread (8 a.m.)	refried beans, tortillas, *guisado* (stew), salsa (9–11 a.m.)	green beans, eggs, beans, agua fresca, soda (4 p.m.)	coffee, bread (9 p.m.)

Note: *Estimated times of meals are included where they were provided by the families.*

open-air kitchens with fires for cooking and toasting foods remain the norm and are described as critical for properly making foods such as tortillas (Ayora-Diaz 2015).

Though many changes in people's choices around eating and the technology they use in the kitchen are limited by structural poverty and the burdens of the past, there are opportunities to eat differently, even with an emphasis on the traditional foods of the region. Compare Señora Genevieve Moreno's description of eating in the past with Doña Ivanna's description of breakfast in the present. Señora Genevieve (San Lorenzo, June 2008) noted that in the past, "people lived different lives, they would eat broth, bread, and chocolate [cocoa]. It was that way for many years. Poor people only ate meat on Sundays—the best day for living life."

Focused on the present, conversely, Doña Ivanna (Zimatlán, July 2008) noted that her children eat the very same foods, "bread, chocolate, coffee, and *atole* [a hot drink made with *maíz*]," but with this list she was describing only breakfast, one of several meals that she prepared in a day. Her children also ate what she called "American dishes"—pizza and hot dogs—as opposed to local dishes that she described as "healthy, like beans, rice, *maíz*, elote, other vegetables, chicken, tamales, *mole amarillo* [yellow mole] and *caldo*."

Household food choices today are not just a matter of region; they reflect foods' classification, quality, and cost. Señora Reyna Pérez (Zimatlán, June 2008) captured the complexity of food choices as she described a typical start to the day: "We will eat *enfrijoladas, entomatadas, huevos estrellados, huevos rancheros, albóndigas de garbanzos*, soup, milk, atole, and oats." Genevieve, too, spoke of breakfast foods, describing *huevos a la mexicana* (scrambled eggs with salsa, onions, and chiles) as a classic American dish that is common in her house. When we asked why *huevos a la mexicana* was considered a classic American dish, she responded that while it is delicious and popular in her home, it is big, the scrambled eggs are in a style that is not Mexican, and the entire dish is prepared with oil, making it rather rich. (These qualities are arguably common to both US and Mexican breakfast foods.) Finally, even though poverty limits what a person might be able to access and afford, it does not limit the creativity they bring to cooking, the aspirations they hold, or the special moments that show up from time to time, particularly around celebrations that allow a limited opportunity to eat differently.

For many of our informants, *mole negro* (black mole) held a special place. It is a dish most often served around holidays and important events (particularly weddings and fiestas). Reyna Pérez described this costly, time-consuming but beloved dish, which for her means it is time to celebrate:

> To prepare mole you need chile ancho, *pasilla mexicana* [a local chile], guajillo chiles, sesame, raisins, galletas Maria [cookies], plantain or plantain castile [a specific variety of plantain], almonds, chocolate, cinnamon, thyme, oregano, cloves, peppers, a little butter, roasted garlic, salt, roasted onion, ground tomato, oil, bay leaf, and a few peanuts.
>
> Once you roast and char the chiles, toast and add garlic, almond, peanuts, sesame, onion . . . all the ingredients that can be toasted, then you put the roasted ingredients in water to remove

the smoke and mix them together. Add more chiles and chocolate and adjust for taste. Next comes the ground tomato and chicken or pork broth, then salt. If you want spicy mole, add more chile, and if you want a sweeter mole, add more chocolate. You can also add more chile and chocolate depending on which mole you are preparing, red mole or black mole. When all the ingredients are added to the mole, mix it again and put it over chicken to eat.

The foods described by our informants beg the question: Where are the chapulines? It is easy to assume that when Oaxacans eat chapulines, their choice reflects the chapulines' ubiquity and status as a well-known and beloved food in the central valleys, their place as a staple food for rural Oaxacans, and their relatively low cost, particularly for the women who produce, harvest, and sell them. Yet, as noted, chapulines are commonly eaten as a snack, and while they can be a main dish, they rarely appear as a central feature on the table. Additionally, while chapulines were an important protein before the arrival of the Spanish, there are many other proteins for locals to choose from in the present, ranging from well-recognized local favorites to newly introduced specialties (including sushi, now available in the city). Finally, though chapulines are relatively inexpensive for growers, harvesters, and chapulineras, they can be costly for consumers. Nevertheless, price is not the only variable that affects choice and eating. Seasonality, demand, ritual needs, and tradition affect how and when chapulines are eaten.

There are many times when chapulines are not the first or even second choice for a local. Out of season, they are not available. At other times of the year, people reject them and insist on a range of other possibilities. So, too, do chapulineras sometimes set aside their chapulines and instead ask their children and families to make alternative choices that will leave the chapulines to be sold (figure 3.2). In other words, the choices people make are not limited to what might be defined as traditional, local, and cheap. Many families are keen to try new foods and new dishes.

Reyna Pérez followed a simple diet, purchasing nearly all her foodstuffs in the Zimatlán market; she had two kitchens and used various appliances and, in particular, a blender almost every day. She regularly used her stove for cooking, kept produce and fruit fresh in her refrigerator, and was learning to prepare turkey in the oven. And still, she

FIGURE 3.2. *Chapulinera, Tlacolula, Chapulines* en venta *(for sale)*. Photo by author.

expressed the hope of learning how to cook new dishes, sharing that she and her family "are always ready to try new foods and new recipes. One recipe I really want to try is chicken with orange sauce."

Amanda García (Zimatlán, July 2008), Doña Ivanna's daughter and a market vendor who sells vegetables, fruit, and some chapulines, is partial to pasta dishes. She recounted her favorite recipe:

> To make pasta, first I prepare the sauce. I grind *yerba santa* [an herb], garlic cloves, pepper, and guajillo chiles with water in the *molcajete* [mortar and pestle]. Then I put the water on to boil the spaghetti. I save some of the water to add to my sauce. Next, I wash the chicken breast and put it in aluminum foil to cook with more *yerba santa*, green chiles, and *quesillo* [cheese]. I put the stuffed breasts wrapped in foil on the stove to steam for about an hour. I also prepare fresh tortillas with *nixtamal* [corn kernels] and lime that comes from the *molinero* [miller] to complete the meal.

Sometimes the choices an individual makes are not about the food but rather about its flavor, spice, and heat. Not everyone is adventurous. Señora Lorena Muñoz complained, "My husband, who is Zapotec, does not eat spicy foods," in sharp contrast to her preferences and her children's choices.[4] She explained: "I like to eat fish, and my husband does not. I like mole that is spicy. But I make it sweet for him; it is harder to prepare, and my children prefer the spice, but he likes it sweet." Young children will often ask for sweet, ready-made, and ultra-processed foods, rejecting "classic" flavors and dishes over taste and chew preferences, even while older children, adults, and seniors choose handmade, unsweetened options (Liem and Mennella 2002; Pérez-Tepayo et al. 2020).

What is perhaps surprising are the limited ways in which chapulines are included in each of these examples. Chapulines can be sautéed with garlic, onions, and vegetables, or mixed with rice and cheese and used for stuffing *chiles rellenos*, but in general, they are eaten by hand directly from bowls as a snack or sometimes rolled into a tortilla and sprinkled with salsa. No one described them as a main dish, even though they are far from unpopular (Hernández Ramírez 2023).

Consumption of chapulines, particularly among Oaxacans over eighteen years of age, reflects three intertwined factors: They are an appetizing snack, with their tasty combination of grasshopper, garlic, lemon, and chile; they are a part of Oaxacan life, something that people know, enjoy, and don't have to think about; and they are a good source of protein (Hernández Ramírez et al. 2021). In recent years, more and more chapulineras and Oaxacans have recited the value of chapulines as a source of protein and praised their purity. Chapulines are safe, clean, and quite nutritious. A 100-gram serving averages about 110 calories, 5 grams of carbohydrates and fat, and 14 grams of protein. In addition, they are rich in vitamins A and C, calcium, iron, and zinc, while free of cholesterol and sugars (Abril et al. 2022; Cerritos and Cano-Santana 2008).

Contemporary consumption of chapulines may have its roots in ancient traditions, but it is not founded on those traditions. Nevertheless, many guides and restauranteurs make a direct and strong connection between the historical and contemporary consumption of chapulines. The stories they tell paint a picture of chapulineras as the granddaughters of an idyllic Indigenous world defined by plenty, celebrated as safe, and marked by a balanced, humane approach to life. Putting aside this imagined history is difficult, but it allows us to better understand the choices contemporary consumers make as they pick chapulines to eat, as well as the factors that constrain their choices.

History and traditional practices may influence the choices made, but they remain choices. While chapulines were a choice before and after the arrival of Europeans to the region, once the region became a colony, the importation of cattle fundamentally changed the diet, altered the dynamics of eating, and imposed new assumptions about race and Indigeneity that tended to disparage Indigenous foods and influence decision-making. In other words, while contemporary Oaxacans may eat some of the same foods that their ancestors consumed, they do not eat them in the same ways.

―― CHAPTER 4 ――
THE CHAPULINES EXPERIENCE

> As for chapulines, they can be crunchy, salty or spicy, but I can now report: they don't taste like chicken.
> —NAT KRIEGER, *SAN DIEGO FREE PRESS*, 2018

> Chock-full of protein, chapulines have been a menu staple in Oaxaca for at least five millennia. Conveniently, chapulines love hanging out among Mexico's principal crops—squash, corn, and beans—and before Spanish colonizers introduced domesticated animals to Mexico in the 16th century, chapulines served as a primary source of protein for people in the region.
> —LIZ WESLANDER, *TRAVEL AWAITS*, 2019

Whether chapulines are rolled into tacos, blended into salsa, or piled into a bowl to be eaten by hand, they are welcomed in the Oaxacan home. Chapulines are an everyday treat that is especially popular around celebrations. Sold by the bag at sporting events and concerts, they are just as popular as popcorn.

The enthusiasm that fills rural Oaxacans at the start of the chapulines season inspires chapulineras. However, locals are not the only people in Oaxaca consuming chapulines, and the discussion of chapulines would not be complete without an acknowledgment of their growing importance for outsiders (foodies, tourists, and others) visiting the region. Oaxaca and Oaxaca City are increasingly popular destinations. Tourism is critical to the state and drives much of the city's economy.[1] Oaxaca is more than its capital city, and most tours include visits to archaeological sites (Monte Albán and Mitla), rural and Indigenous artisanal communities, and the region's many markets (Ruiz et al. 2021).

Walking the city is a good way to experience Oaxaca and gain a sense of its history and significance. It is also one of the ways that guides can create and promote its symbolic status and value as a unique place (Barrera-Fernández and Hernández-Escampa 2017). The goal for most guides is not to teach an academic version of Oaxaca's history that takes account of the brutality of the conquest, colonialism, revolution, and contemporary resistance. Rather, most guides sell an experience that brings the past together with the present in the creation of something special (Le et al. 2019; Ramos-García 2023).

The Oaxaca experience develops as guides, hoteliers, restauranteurs, and local entrepreneurs and artisans host outsiders. Their goal is to make the visitor comfortable, safe, and secure while earning a living. Comfort comes in many forms, including food that is edible and water that is clean. Inequality and insecurity, health threats, and the misperception of what is safe to consume complicate eating for unprepared outsiders, leaving chapulines (among other local food traditions) in an odd position between edible and inedible. Managing the perceived risks (whether real or imagined) is a difficult job, yet for restauranteurs, hoteliers, and guides, it is critical to their success (Ayieko et al. 2021; Hwang and Choe 2020; Youssef and Spence 2021).

An uncomplicated way for outsiders to experience chapulines and leave their phobia behind is to eat them as an appetizer. Served with a shot of mezcal and alongside tortillas and salsa, chapulines are simple, safe, and even quotidian. In fact, served first with more common fare like salsa and chips, they become a minor element in a series of foods that define Oaxacan foodways.[2] While this encounter can satisfy most outsiders, the more adventurous visitor can look beyond restaurant offerings and enter the marketplace in search of chapulines in situ. This quest might risk their health and well-being (so say the guidebooks), but the opportunity to satisfy their curiosity, have an authentic experience, and show their strength when confronted with unfamiliar, seemingly inedible food is an important event in itself (Gyimóthy and Mykletun 2009; Mkono 2011).

Claude Lévi-Strauss (1963) argued that totems (fetishized symbols that stand for and represent groups of people) are critical to forming an identity and organizing a worldview. Our social relationships with others are maintained through the totems we associate with and use to identify insiders and outsiders. When totems are based on food symbols, whether edible or inedible, they nourish both body and mind, consolidating what we know and what we fear. By this logic, we can paraphrase Lévi-Strauss and argue that chapulines are good to think about and good to eat, fulfilling different roles for locals and outsiders. The critical differences in the ways outsiders and local Oaxacans approach, consume, and think about chapulines can be tracked along four key themes.

First, locals and outsiders value chapulines differently. For locals, chapulines are food, something to be eaten. Outsiders, on the other hand, fetishize chapulines as symbols and commodify them as valuable signs of the past. Second, this fetishizing by outsiders renders the status of chapulines as an everyday food problematic. Locals may consume them, but they are special for outsiders, who cannot connect the insects to a daily routine. Locals approach chapulines as food and worry about how much they cost and how they will fit into a food budget. Outsiders, focused on having an experience, are unconcerned with costs and the everyday value of chapulines. They are interested in experiencing what their guidebooks and popular histories of the region recommend. Third, due to the fetishizing by outsiders, the economic value of chapulines to the local community and their importance to chapulineras are masked. The struggles that confront chapulineras in the marketplace are not important for outsiders, who are seeking to experience Oaxaca. Fourth, with an interest in an imagined Oaxaca, outsiders are searching for a way to experience an identity that is founded in the mythical representation of a pre-Columbian past (Hepp 2019). While chapulineras and locals negotiate sales and prepare meals, restauranteurs and guides use chapulines to create a present that is rooted in the fantasy of an ancient and Indigenous Oaxaca.

Appearing alongside chocolate, mole, and mezcal, chapulines are part of the suite of foods that are collectively referenced as "food of the gods" by popular media, in celebration of Oaxaca's rich culinary history.[3] Guides, restauranteurs, travel writers, and others use this phrase in association with regular tours to celebrate and capitalize on local foodways. The ongoing association of common foods with mythical, spiritual possibilities elevates them to the status of something special. It highlights their rich qualities and creates connections to other special, appetizing delicacies from around the globe, including, among other treats, expensive cheeses, truffles, caviar, and foie gras.

Exoticized, chapulines are transformed from a food that belongs to the masses into sought-after haute cuisine. Fetishized as symbol rather than food source, chapulines are repositioned as "metaphysical subtleties and theological niceties" (Marx [1867] 1992, 163). In other words, chapulines are transformed from food to feature, and eating becomes an experience that is spiritual rather than nutritional. References to "food of the gods" include notes on tours and restaurants as well as the (no longer held) annual celebration of heritage cooking, which ran for about a decade in the early 2000s.[4]

Chapulines, represented as "food of the gods," gain symbolic value. The honorific acknowledges the history of native cuisines in Oaxaca, the role that ancestral chefs played in the preservation of life, and an ethical way of living that celebrates nature. These assumptions of what mattered in the past are deemed important to the present by outsiders and the state. In fact, chapulines reimagined as haute cuisine and "food of the gods" confound locals. Chapulineras are happy to exploit the opportunity and sell chapulines to outsiders. They are also ready to embellish their own stories of production; nevertheless, the sales made by chapulineras to outsiders remain small, infrequent, and largely inconsequential.

Rural and Indigenous Oaxacans approach chapulines as food first. Chapulines are neither glamorous nor particularly exotic. Restauranteurs reimagine chapulines in terms of a uniquely Western take and wrap the "inedible" insect in history, sustainability, and spirituality. Fetishized and appropriated by restauranteurs, chapulines are used in myriad ways. Beyond serving them, businesses make direct references to chapulines and use them symbolically in advertising and promotions. In many cases, chapulines are logos. Sometimes the logo is nothing more than an image of a grasshopper pasted onto a billboard, creating an unspoken connection to place and past, or what Sherry B. Ortner (1973, 1339) called a summarizing symbol.

The figure of a *chapulín* also appears in restaurants, small grocery stores, and galleries in reference to local traditions, signifying authenticity and the insects' status as a relic of the past. In each of these examples, the symbolic use of chapulines is focused on the outsider and is central to their experience of Oaxaca. For the outsider, the symbol makes a connection to a local producer or artisan, but rather than conveying a concern with nutrition, good health, or inequality, the symbol suggests the past. Connecting entrepreneurs who reside in the city with chapulineras in the countryside accomplishes two important goals. It drives economic growth and fosters sustainability, as outsiders come to regard chapulines as a normal part of the diet (see also Tomassini 2021). While chapulineras earn little from restauranteurs and even less from foodies and tourists visiting the region, working with businesses in the city creates demand and increases competition for outsiders' money. A positive outcome for all, increased demand and increased incomes encourage economic growth. Problematically, the results in Oaxaca are a two-tiered economic system that places a premium on meeting the needs of outsiders while ignoring the needs of the local population (Gullette 2007; Matute 2021; Ramos-García et al. 2023).

The complex meaning of chapulines is further complicated, as they are used to connect contemporary life to the past. With a focus on creating compelling stories for outsiders, chapulines are part of a fantasy and linked to a mythical, rustic past, or *un espacio único y acogedor, donde podrás disfrutar de la magia y el encanto de Oaxaca* (a unique and welcoming space, where you can enjoy the magic and charm of Oaxaca). Los Chapulineros, Oaxaca's professional soccer team, playing in La Liga de Balompié Mexicano since 2020, has as its motto *Somos Chapulineros, Somos Oaxaca* (We are Chapulineros, We are Oaxaca). The slogan argues for a collective identity for the region, yet leaves unacknowledged the social inequalities that separate urban and rural communities and ignores the efforts of "real" chapulineras.

Many of the more complex constructions using chapulines in advertising and promotions make historical connections between the present day and the region's deep history as the homeland of Mixe, Mixtec, and Zapotec. In these examples, chapulines are a symbol of ancient culinary foodways. Using a broad brush, local guides, guidebooks, and social media sweep together unique and independent Indigenous groups, often avoiding any discussion of the temporal, geographic, linguistic, and cultural differences that separate them. In other words, rather than focus on what makes Zapotec, Mixtec, and Mixe different, this narrative lumps all Indigenous peoples together and creates a history that amplifies the mythology of contemporary consumption. Chapulines are promoted as a taste of the past rooted in ancient rituals and practices, while contemporary consumption is simply a continuation of that past.[5] Finally, guides use tours and tales focused on chapulines to celebrate Oaxacan resilience and note how local populations adapted to the conquest and the food changes it brought.[6]

The fetishized representations of chapulines are not necessarily wrong. However, they do misrepresent how chapulines are used and consumed by Indigenous and rural Oaxacans. More importantly, the misrepresentations challenge the status of locals, who are forced to define themselves in response to fantastic and unacceptable interpretations. Beholden to an imagined past, chapulines are not part of the present. It also means that the discrimination, inequality, and poverty that confront most rural and Indigenous Oaxacans are minimized, as they are celebrated for their ancestry rather than their experiences in the present (Ramos-García et al. 2023).

Chapulineras face new challenges in the marketplace when chapulines are commodified, fetishized, and appropriated. Chapulineras know how to play into the desire of outsiders who want to meet and buy from the descendants of Oaxaca's major Indigenous groups. They present chapulines as an ancient food and regularly recount the dietary benefits they hold as a high-protein, low-calorie food. Nevertheless, the downplaying of the realities of everyday life means that the marketplace becomes a caricature of the challenges chapulineras face as they manage clients, work with restauranteurs, and engage with outsiders.

Their business efforts contrast with and often contradict the viewpoint of outsiders, who are drawn to an imagined ideal of what the chapulines represent. These outsiders do not see chapulineras' success, the intensity of their efforts, or the ways they juggle responsibilities and adapt in moments of crisis (Cook and Crang 1996). Without a grasp on the efforts of chapulineras and the environmental crises and social inequalities that surround and affect production and consumption, outsiders cannot understand how overharvesting, contamination and pesticide use, pandemics, habitat loss, climate change, poverty, and food insecurity affect meaning and value (Cohen and Mata-Sánchez 2021).

Fetishizing chapulines also divorces them from their role in community life. Describing them as "food of the gods" and connecting them to an imagined history creates a vacuum where no meaning exists; filling this vacuum are mythical representations that imply that chapulines are a rare luxury from the past, something only available to the privileged few. Chapulines in this description are not accessible and common. Outsiders are eating "food of the gods," not food for the masses or food that is a critical part of the Oaxacan diet and crucial to chapulineras' economic well-being.

Foodies, guides, guidebooks, and restauranteurs embrace eating chapulines as a dare (Mkono 2011). A dare food breaks the rules of consumption for the eater. For Westerners, chapulines are a dare food that demands that the consumer suspend judgment and try something that, according to the rules of eating, is dangerous and inedible. It makes no sense to eat an insect. In fact, eating insects carries a sense of contamination and disgust. Eating a food that engenders disgust is not easy. Eating something that is thought to be inedible, disgusting, dirty, or dangerous demands that the eater suspend the sociocultural rules that have guided consumption through time. But the challenge around chapulines is complicated by the simple fact that for most Oaxacans in the central valleys, they are commonly consumed. While chapulines are a dare for outsiders, they are a regular dish for locals. The disconnect can be profound, as outsiders and eaters from afar doubt the reality of a system that would deny social norms and embrace the yuckiness of the food in question, so much so that the food is part of the everyday diet. In other words, while outsiders may be ready to eat chapulines, they are not likely able to make sense of the chapulines' value, meaning, and place in the local diet.

Outsiders are not interested in the dynamics of the marketplace or the economic forces that define the proteins available to locals. Outsiders must overcome their disgust, and restauranteurs are happy to oblige. They mention celebrities, reference the past, and play up the strength and bravery of the consumer (Legendre and Baker 2021). Outsiders to the region are seeking to celebrate themselves and escape the everyday; they are not necessarily interested in meaning. Nevertheless, to assume that chapulines are a holdover or sign of the past advances a myth that relegates chapulineras to the margins and limits an understanding of their value and importance in the present (Escalante-Aburto et al. 2022).

Eating chapulines is a social act informed by cultural traditions that are real (everyday eating), imagined (pre-Columbian eating), and invented ("food of the gods"). For locals, chapulines are a regular part of the diet and a highly anticipated seasonal treat that reflects and responds to social status, taste, and traditional practices. Locals' love for chapulines is the culmination of these forces over time. For outsiders, chapulines are a rare delicacy and dare. Their seasonality is not a concern. A trip to Oaxaca covers a few days or weeks and may be part of a longer visit to other parts of Mexico. Because both the tourist season and chapulines season largely come in the summer months, visitors imagine that there are always chapulines available (see Goertzen 2010).[7]

The disinterest of visitors in the everyday challenges that Oaxacans face as they put together meals, pay for groceries, deal with the vagaries of the market, and cope with the climate's effect on agriculture is typical of the tourist gaze (Choe and Lugosi 2023). While a vacation is an opportunity to "get away" and relax, it obscures the social inequalities and discrimination that confront local people daily and contribute to their overall marginalization. Restauranteurs and guides do not dwell on these issues, and visitors are likely left unaware of the importance of chapulines for locals or for the chapulineras who depend on them.

Fetishized, chapulines are repositioned in the diet and their material value is ignored. Chapulines become an experience for outsiders that reflects an imagined past based on mythical assumptions that include a sense of natural balance and wholesome integration, ignoring their role as a part of the daily diet. The marketplace where people go to find their chapulines and other foods no longer matters. The reality of the marketplace as a destination critical to everyday life cannot compete with its presentation as a holdover from the past: a chaotic celebration of noise, color, flavors, and aromas.[8]

In this fantastic misrepresentation of chapulines, chapulineras are not successful entrepreneurs, but representatives of Oaxaca's rural poor, assumed to be Indigenous and working to supplement their husbands' proper efforts to support their families (Gamlin 2020; Nova 2003). While chapulineras are often rural, the poverty that surrounds them is not congenital; it is a part of the marginalization and precarity that have plagued the region for generations. Furthermore, most chapulineras are not Indigenous. While many acknowledge that their parents or grandparents were members of ethnic minorities in Oaxaca, they typically use the term *mestiza* or simply oaxaqueña to refer to themselves. Critically, the ease with which chapulineras do their jobs facilitates describing their

Table 4.1. Chapulineras' Control over Sales of Chapulines

	Who decides how to sell (%)	Who decides where to sell (%)	Who controls sales income (%)
self (independently)	88	88	86
self/husband	12	10	4
self/family		2	8
other (wholesalers)			2

work as a supplement to their husbands' efforts. Yet this assumption could not be more problematic. More than 85 percent of chapulineras work for themselves, deciding where to sell and exercising control over their incomes.

The assumption that families or husbands control chapulineras and always influence their decision-making is simply wrong (see table 4.1). Yet this misconception leads to a series of assumptions that are pervasive in the analysis of rural and Indigenous women in Latin America. These assumptions rob chapulineras of their autonomy as social beings working in the marketplace, suggesting that the work they do is not central to household reproduction but rather reflects traditions dating back some three thousand to five thousand years. Perhaps most damaging, these assumptions conceal the successes many chapulineras enjoy and present their efforts as failing, when in reality they are doing very well (see also Gross 2011).

The imagined chapulinera looks something like this: a young woman in a simple cotton dress, with braided hair and a gingham apron. She carries her chapulines through the market in a large, handwoven basket. Selling chapulines, she represents a series of "multiple nostalgias" that create an image of Oaxaca and rural Oaxacan women that is mystical and mythic (Poole 2004). The magical quality of Oaxaca is repeated in the displays of freshly prepared chapulines, other vegetables, and dry goods—including corn husks for wrapping tamales—that are ready for use and consumption. The outsider may purchase a sample of any of these items to enjoy, but it is a curiosity. Few, if any, outsiders are looking for groceries, and many will read the marketplace as chaotic and dangerous. Misreading chapulineras and the marketplace effectively dislocates their efforts from the present and divorces them from the local economy.

The misrepresentation of chapulines limits the recognition of the social inequalities and discrimination reproduced in the diet. Chapulines are food for rural Oaxacans and a reflection of the social inequalities that confront most poor, rural, and Indigenous Oaxacans and separate them from their more well-off urban neighbors. Without the resources to buy food or access to well-stocked, reasonably priced food markets, most rural and Indigenous Oaxacans confront food insecurity daily (Gladstone 2023; Martínez-Martínez et al. 2023; Novotny et al. 2021).

Bluntly put, the dislocation does more than simply mystify the meaning of chapulines. It suggests that chapulineras are best thought of as following an ancient set of practices that they have managed into the present. Chapulines may be a practical, well-known, and regular part of daily life, but they are not what "modern" consumers would choose, and while their unique quality enhances their status for outsiders as something different, it limits an understanding of the role they play in the region.

For rural and Indigenous Oaxacans, chapulines are a welcome part of meals, a delicious snack, and a signifier of springtime. Their meaning is different for visitors to the region. Outsiders tend to ignore the role of chapulines in daily life and approach them as a marker of Indigeneity, a chance to eat the "food of the gods." The separation between these two models (one of use, the other of meaning) complicates the role of chapulines in the construction of local identity. In effect, for rural and Indigenous Oaxacans, an identity emerges through their daily consumption of chapulines as well as the insects' place on the kitchen table. This identity contrasts and conflicts with the fetishized chapulines that outsiders embrace as they connect with an imagined and mythical past.

The misrepresentations that surround both chapulines and chapulineras limit an understanding of the instrumental role they play in the local diet and economy, pointing instead toward an approach to identity and belonging that is phenotypic and ignores the surrounding world system. The symbolic reinterpretation of chapulines is not concerned with eating in the present; rather, the goal is to discover eating in the past. Fetishized and appropriated by visitors who are interested in experience, authenticity, and tradition, chapulines are a celebrated yet anachronistic delicacy. They are accessible to outsiders, but the social inequalities that surround their harvest, production, and use are missed or misrepresented.

Identity is not in question for Oaxacans, as they choose to eat chapulines. Chapulines satisfy hunger, and they are economical and abundant. The pleasure and satisfaction they bring is not about meeting an abstract concern for protein or arriving at a place where past meets present; it is about living in the moment and experiencing the hope that accompanies every spring as the rains usher in a new growing season in anticipation of successes. Oaxacans cherish chapulines.

Like their Oaxacan hosts, visitors are driven by more than dietary necessity in their choice to eat chapulines. The choice is about identity, but in this case, it is the individual's identity, not the group's. Electing to eat chapulines is an opportunity to show off, to be in control of one's gag reflex, and to contradict the disgust that is typically associated with the thought of consuming "inedible" insects. Chapulines are an experience, and eating an insect is a way to set oneself apart. In other words, trying chapulines is not expressly about eating; it is about virtue eating. Virtue eating, like virtue signaling, gives the consumer the opportunity to demonstrate their care, depth, and understanding, even as it is also critiqued as a kind of symbolic allyship. The practice of eating chapulines is used to prove dedication, understanding, and a willingness to push beyond the limits of entomophobia in order to connect with the Other (De Souza 2019). It is the moment when the outsider transcends boundaries and lives up to the local saying, "If you eat a *chapulín*, you will always return to Oaxaca." Grounded in the imagined histories of the region that fill guidebooks, websites, and city tours, it is an exciting moment that builds on visits to archaeological sites, colonial monuments, museums, parks, markets, rural communities, and natural wonders, as well as the consumption of lots of other foods.[9]

To be captivated by an imagined past and to embrace an identity as an exceptionally brave consumer does not mean that outsiders follow false trails or fictional stories. Rather, they are practicing an identity that is not so much connected to a version of contemporary Oaxaca as it is to the expectations of something special. It is rooted in assumptions about the past and experiences in the present that share little with the efforts of rural and Indigenous Oaxacans. Outsiders play up the mystical and spiritual, emphasizing the ancestral ingredients that make Oaxaca special, while downplaying local practice and ignoring the social inequalities, discrimination, and violence that confront the Indigenous and rural poor.

This is particularly clear in discussions of contemporary life that limit stories of brutality and instead imagine the region as a bucolic and peaceful homeland to native peoples. In this telling, the place of chapulines as a special food is exaggerated, and both their traditional role as a critical protein source and their unique, non-Western qualities in the present are emphasized (Bérubé and Forde 2024).

Popular stories of Oaxaca's traditional foodways assume that food choices passively reflect social practice, ritual life, and community. Yet what people eat does more than reproduce and reflect identities. Foodways are critical arenas in which people negotiate their world, make sense of social organization, and change why some things matter. Celebrations, cooperation, and spirituality are certainly part of the food traditions in Oaxaca. However, food is much more. John Edward Staller and Michael Carrasco (2010) note that foodways often determine ritual practices and influence social organization around the home, the marketplace, and the community.

An alternative pathway to understanding the history of foodways in Oaxaca is to focus on how the consumption of chapulines reflects four core assumptions that outsiders make about Indigenous peoples. First, they assume that all rural Oaxacans—and therefore all chapulineras—are Indigenous. Second, they approach Oaxacan Indigeneity as something mystical, reflected in enigmatic places like Monte Albán and Mitla. Indigeneity is the antithesis of the urbane and the Western, and it is defined by a lifestyle and worldview that remain removed and isolated from the larger world. Third, they see the decline of Indigenous Oaxaca since the conquest as confirmation of the weakness of today's communities. And fourth, they believe that it is possible to experience Indigenous life, in service of which visitors seek out guides, tours, and experiential programs (including cooking programs) that will give them the opportunity to participate in local rituals and fiestas (Goertzen 2010).

Guides, programs, and tours offer one version of life in Oaxaca. The issue is not the relative accuracy of this version but, rather, its centering of a mythical narrative that leaves unacknowledged the realities of daily life—the social inequalities and injustices that define the lives of the rural poor. Furthermore, assuming that Oaxacan identities are rooted in ethnicity, and founded in a pre-Columbian, Indigenous past, creates a version of the contemporary world that assumes that most rural Oaxacans are Indigenous.

Oaxacans have diverse backgrounds that include not just multiple Indigenous communities but also Afro-Caribbeans and Middle Eastern immigrants who arrived in the state over a century ago, as well as a large community of undocumented migrants from Nicaragua, Guatemala, and Honduras who have settled in the city more recently. That diversity is found among chapulineras. In fact, only about 7 percent of the women interviewed in 2022 identified as Indigenous. The overwhelming majority acknowledged that while they might have ancestral roots in a rural, Indian community, they were mestiza and part of modern Mexico. While the history of Oaxaca is rooted in the Indigenous past of the region, it was not some mythical peaceful world but a world defined by violence and conquest. That violence shifted with the arrival of the Spanish, but it did not end. And after the colonial period gave way to Mexico, new forms of discrimination arose (Matute 2021).

Rural and Indigenous peoples in Oaxaca do not live in isolation from the nation that surrounds them. They are a product of the nation and its history, and while they are often poor, poverty is not destiny or an innate part of what it means to be Indigenous. Rather, it is an outcome of the many inequalities that rural folks face daily, including limited schooling, health care, access to resources, and access to opportunities (see Cohen 1999).

A mountain of chapulines in the marketplace is a special sight. Easily fetishized, its value can be exaggerated and embellished. This is particularly the case for visitors to Oaxaca, who have no gauge with which to measure the worth and status of what they are seeing. Mountains of chapulines are valuable, but not because they are rare and great for local folks who need to depend on tourism and tourist dollars to support them. Tourism brings a great deal to the state, but mountains of chapulines for sale to outsiders and nonlocals do little to help chapulineras or mitigate the global economic forces and social inequalities that are at work in Oaxaca. Assumptions by outsiders are a challenge to chapulineras, misrepresenting these women's identity and suggesting that it is rooted in ancient and Indigenous traditions.

Assumed Indigeneity and a commitment to authenticity frame how outsiders, restauranteurs, foodies, and tourists approach the experience of eating. Chapulines are not food for them, but a symbol of that experience. Defined as symbol rather than food, chapulines are not a part of everyday life. In contrast, chapulineras and the rural folks they serve are focused on the materiality of the chapulines, not their symbolic value as fetish. Yet understanding how they are fetishized, their value in daily life, their materiality, and their complicated relationship to identity reveals their complexities and moves us beyond Jean Anthelme Brillat-Savarin's (1999, 3) well-worn saying, "Tell me what you eat, and I will tell you who you are."

PART III
MARKETING CHAPULINES

—— CHAPTER 5 ——
HOW TO SELL CHAPULINES IN OAXACA

Chapulines, sometimes they are fifty pesos and sometimes one hundred pesos, but it is determined by their size. I like buying them alive and cleaned, so there is not as much junk to separate.
—DOÑA ADRIANA RUIZ, MERCADO LA MERCED, OAXACA, 2022

I make sales every day. There are days when I sell everything and others when I don't. But during the season and when the chapulines are full-grown in October, that is when my sales are best.
—ROSA ALTAMIRANO, OCOTLÁN, 2008

Chapulines are at the heart of a thriving economy. Vendors set up their products in stalls and between aisles in markets large and small, including the Mercado la Merced, the Mercado Benito Juárez, and the Mercado 20 de Noviembre; at regional weekly markets; and at the Centro de Abastos, home to retailers and wholesalers who supply much of the food for the city's restaurants.

Chapulineras make their names and create reputations through the strength of their relationships with their clients, as well as their unerring ability to fill orders and meet deadlines, no matter the constraints. There is little formal advertising around the marketplace for grasshoppers; instead, chapulineras rely on word of mouth, social media (including posts on Facebook groups like Chapulines Oaxaqueños and Chapulines en

Venta), and the small flow of restauranteurs and tourists to succeed. The most important indicator of a chapulinera's success is positive word of mouth from her clients. Their trust and repeated business are evidence of her experience and preparation. The connection brings clients back year after year, whether they are interested in an order delivered locally or one for export across the Mexico-US border.

Tourism accounts for approximately 30 percent of the state's economy. Tourism's importance to the economic well-being of the city overshadows the value of chapulines (see Goertzen 2010). There is growing demand for chapulines by high-end restaurants that cater to outsiders and foodies; nevertheless, that demand is not as critical to chapulineras as is the local market. The rise in demand for chapulines in the tourism-related market is cyclical and minor in contrast to daily sales. It is largely oriented around specific events that attract outsiders (tourists and nonlocals) amid the chapulines season—including the Guelaguetza celebration in early July and Día de los Muertos (Day of the Dead), a celebratory period that runs from October 31 to November 6 (see also Haley and Fukuda 2014; Whitford 2009). In the words of Doña Adriana, "foreigners buy, but they are here on holiday. At the moment [late May 2023] there are more tourists, so there are restaurant owners visiting as well."

Chapulineras are independent and happy with the state of their market, unlike *mezcaleros* (those capitalizing on the growing popularity of mezcal), *artesanos* (craftspeople), and gallery owners, all of whom often work with investors to grow their businesses and meet external demand. Chapulineras are not interested in working with promoters or outsiders who want to invest and grow their market (Arellano-Plaza et al. 2022; Lira et al. 2022). Chapulineras cater to local clients and plan for the local marketplace. They know that their hard work and attention to their clientele will carry them forward. Chapulineras emphasize fulfilling the requests of clients, and they are laser focused on their mission.

It is easy to miss just how attuned chapulineras are to the needs of their clients when one encounters a vendor in the market. Set up with her chapulines, she appears isolated and concerned with the day: Will she make her sales? With only the occasional shopper stopping to chat and to taste and buy a handful of chapulines, the chances to succeed appear slim. But she is on her phone, checking with her suppliers and working with clients, intent on finishing sales. It may not be apparent, but she is busy negotiating, organizing, and filling orders. In fact, she is not in the market looking for sales that she does not have; rather, she is in the market to capture supplemental sales and earn a little extra while fulfilling regular orders. Selling to outsiders and visitors in the market is merely a way in which she can earn a little more. And if the consumers that she meets in the moment become regular clients, it is all the better for her bottom line.

Chapulineras are their own brand, and they do not label their chapulines beyond size and flavor. Terroir is not a critical concern, though they often say disparaging things about vendors from other states. There are chapulineras who have invested in producing freeze-dried, long-preserved chapulines for sale in Oaxaca and through US- and Mexican-based businesses. However, the overwhelming efforts of chapulineras are focused on clients and consumers who want freshly cooked chapulines at fair prices, as well as a supply that will not end abruptly.

Chapulineras know how to work their milpa to support the growth cycle of chapulines and make the most of harvest. Nevertheless, most focus their time and efforts on the marketplace and are willing to buy chapulines when their own fields are limited or empty, or when production demands are high. The former situation arises for those vendors who do not have access to enough milpa to support production in quantities that clients demand. In fact, chapulineras may not hold title to more than a small milpa, and many central valley families own and work plots of less than half a hectare (Cohen 1999). Even with access to neighboring plots and communal lands, production can be limited and force a chapulinera to look to others to fulfill their needs. The latter situation arises because many vendors are selling hundreds of kilograms of chapulines over the course of the season, and intricacies of production can require significant outlays of time. Out of the field, successful chapulineras spend a lot of their time managing client demand and balancing their stock. In the process, chapulineras develop formal relationships with harvesters as they negotiate contracts and establish pathways to access prepared grasshoppers. Sometimes harvesters are small-scale producers who live nearby and are not able to enter the marketplace as vendors; at other times the harvesters come from outside a chapulinera's home village. In either case, the chapulinera and harvester develop a mutually beneficial system that connects them and creates opportunity.

The wholesale cost of chapulines ranges from MXN 50 to MXN 200 per kilogram, depending on size, any processing completed, the addition of flavoring (particularly chile), and the relationship of chapulinera to provider. Connections can influence costs, and some women turn to extended family members, friends, and community connections to lower production costs.

For some harvesters, the sale of chapulines is a way to deal with a plague. They are interested in ridding their milpas of grasshoppers, and they know that once collected, a chapulinera will buy what they have. Chapulines threaten the welfare of crops and can reduce a field of *maíz* to short, dead stalks in mere minutes. Sometimes—particularly in cases that put needed fields of maíz at risk of destruction by grasshoppers—the money that changes hands as harvesters sell fresh chapulines to buyers is almost secondary to ridding their fields of a dangerous and destructive insect.

Chapulineras market chapulines in quantities that are overwhelming, and informal estimates suggest that over 350,000 metric tons are produced annually. Many of the women who participate in this study were selling ten to twenty kilograms of chapulines weekly. Given demand, the size of the market, and the need to meet orders quickly, it is not a surprise that chapulineras look beyond their own holdings as they organize chapulines for sale. Nevertheless, they are quite reticent to describe the relationships they have with the people who supply them. Many would talk about harvesting on their own and occasionally contracting with harvesters, but it was difficult to learn how much chapulineras paid suppliers.

There are a few reasons behind the difficulties we encountered as we asked about chapulineras' ability to meet demand and their dependence on harvesters. First, the relationship of chapulineras to harvesters is carefully managed, and talking about incomes can be destabilizing. Second, the mythologies that surround women's work in Oaxaca assume that they are not involved in complex, contractual relationships but are instead merely supplementing critical efforts by the male household head to meet the demands of daily life. Third, few chapulineras trust anyone who might meddle in their market; they are quite circumspect in their descriptions of their work lives (Payne and Van Itterbeeck 2017).

The relationship of chapulinera to supplier is typically contractual and not built on kin ties, dyadic contracts, or the cooperative relationships that are associated with Mesoamerican life (see, e.g., Cohen 1999). A contractual exchange is founded on the assumption of trust between two parties, in this case the chapulinera and her supplier. Their agreement defines their schedule and details delivery of chapulines as well as their preparation. In return, the chapulinera is obligated to pay an agreed-on price. While the successful completion of one contract can lead to more, chapulineras can and do jump from one harvester to another. In those moments, chapulineras and their harvesters can negotiate new contracts and fees in response to market seasonality, demand, and the social climate.

For some chapulineras, contracts carry them to growers from outside Oaxaca. Like chapulineras who are always looking for a reliable partner, many growers who bring their chapulines to Oaxaca are looking for dependable regular buyers. Nevertheless, nonlocal growers have reputations as secretive, stubborn, and focused on making sales at any cost, including by selling chapulines that are stale, have not been rested and allowed to fully process any waste, or are contaminated. Further, while vendors in the marketplace might be expected to drop their prices as the day progresses, producers from outside the state are described by chapulineras as unreasonable negotiators. Outside producers, as Señor Julián Ramírez noted (Centro de Abastos, July 2007), will leave the marketplace with unsold chapulines rather than accepting an unreasonable contract.[1]

Many assumptions are made about the capabilities of women in rural Oaxaca that limit their access to the market, work, and entrepreneurism. The treatment of women in the Oaxacan marketplace, and in particular Indigenous and rural women, is marked by discrimination and bigotry (Danielson and Eisenstadt 2009). This is not new; throughout much of the region's history, women have been assumed to lack the skills needed to succeed in business (Karver et al. 2016; Stephen 1991). Amid an authoritative system that presupposes the superiority of men in the public sphere, including the marketplace, women are relegated to providing childcare, managing the home, and caring for their family (Howell 1999). While there were and are clear signs that women can ably manage different jobs and effectively compete with men in the marketplace and beyond, there is little to no space for them to put their talents to work (Familar 2017).

Chapulineras deal with this reality daily. It is not unusual to find men, whether locals or outsiders, who assume they can take advantage of chapulineras. In the marketplace they often ask for special favors, attempt to trick vendors and seize valuable product, and complain when they are forced to simply pay what is asked. My fieldwork team watched this process play out on more than one occasion, as chapulineras negotiated with men who, assuming their own superiority, demanded special attention and lower prices. Sometimes these buyers would accuse the chapulinera of turning her back on her responsibilities to her children and home. These moments never ended well for the potential buyer, who was typically left standing with little or nothing to show for his efforts. It was not hard to see the moment when these men realized that the chapulineras they were trying to manipulate were quite cognizant of what was happening. They know the game and the value of their goods, and they neither panic that a sale may not occur nor succumb to the accusations of insufficient care.

In fact, few chapulineras trust anyone beyond their immediate family, and they are particularly skeptical of outsiders who meddle in their business and try to take advantage of their time and energy. The history of chapulineras in the marketplace is marked by episodes where other vendors, buyers, businessmen, and businesswomen, as well as well-intentioned outsiders, have taken advantage of vendors on the assumption that they lack basic business skills (Canedo 2019).

In some cases, particularly with persistent and well-intentioned outsiders, chapulineras find themselves unable to effectively respond. Violeta Gutiérrez-Zamora (2021, 149) describes this challenge clearly in her work with campesinas and community forestry programming in the southern part of the state. Too often the goals of NGOs and state-supported conservancy programs are based on binary gender models. These programs, which are set up to bring women into income-generating activities, neglect the ways in which such efforts exacerbate long-standing biases and bigotries (see also Cruz-Torres 2012). The mistrust that characterizes the relationships of chapulineras to outsiders mirrors this process. Chapulineras are not struggling rural women at the mercy of the marketplace, yet the assumption that they are reaches deep into both official and popular histories of market women and is obvious in the repeated and overwhelming discrimination that confronts Indigenous and rural folks.

The business of chapulines generates a lot of money. And while sales are not tracked by the state or federal government, we can infer from the data collected for this project that producers are selling thousands of kilograms and earning well in the process. Chapulineras know that their product is valuable.

To determine sales outcomes, we asked chapulineras to track sales through recall and to describe their days in the marketplace. We asked chapulineras to estimate weekly sales, income, and prices charged, as well as to record descriptions of their clientele, among other things.

Chapulineras approach the marketplace in one of four ways: as entrepreneurs, local retailers, wholesalers, or family providers. Entrepreneurs develop relationships that reach beyond their local communities to include clients, restauranteurs, and outsiders, and they typically work from stalls in Oaxaca City markets. Local retailers serve clientele largely within their home communities. Wholesalers fulfill large orders and work from stalls in the marketplace or their homes. Finally, family providers focus on the household and fellow villagers. Table 5.1 summarizes the efforts of chapulineras and their different approaches to the marketplace. Within the table, the four kinds of chapulinera (entrepreneur, local retailer, wholesaler, and family provider) are divided into quartiles. These quartiles segment each approach to sales into four equal groups to capture the complex conduct of chapulineras, which ranges from casual, infrequent smaller sales of a few kilograms to serious, planned sales of tens of kilograms regularly.

Thirty-one of the chapulineras interviewed for this project (53 percent) were entrepreneurs who sold to a diverse clientele of local customers, restauranteurs, and outsiders. Entrepreneurs in quartile 1 sold two to three kilograms daily and approximately eighteen kilograms weekly. Their weekly earnings of MXN 700–1,000 were enough to more than cover everyday expenses. Chapulineras in quartile 2 doubled the output of the first quartile, earning incomes that allowed for more flexibility and covered unanticipated expenses. Those in quartiles 3 and 4, meanwhile, had sales ranging from seven to forty kilograms daily. Their efforts were exceptional, as were their weekly incomes of MXN 2,450–14,000.

Table 5.1. Weekly Sales by Chapulineras, Summer 2022

Entrepreneurs

	Q1	Q2	Q3	Q4
chapulineras (n = 28)	8	8	6	6
range of kgs sold daily	2–3	4–6	7–10	11–40
total kgs sold weekly	18	39	51	151
income range	700–1,050	1,400–2,100	2,450–3,500	3,850–14,000

Local retailers

	Q1	Q2	Q3	Q4
chapulineras (n = 12)	3	3	5	1
range of kgs sold daily	1–2	3–5	5–6	7
total kgs sold weekly	5	12	28	7
income range	350–700	1,050–1,750	1,750–2,100	2,450

Wholesalers

	Q1	Q2	Q3	Q4
chapulineras (n = 9)	2	2	4	1
range of kgs sold daily	1	3–4	5	6
total kgs sold weekly	2	7	20	6
income range	350	1,050–1,400	1,750	2,100

Family providers

	Q1	Q2	Q3	Q4
chapulineras (n = 5)	2	1	1	1
range of kgs sold daily	2	5	7	15
total kgs sold weekly	4	5	7	15
income range	inconsistent sales			

Note: *Sales figures are in kilograms (kgs); income is in Mexican pesos.*

Entrepreneurs tend to work in Oaxaca City's larger markets, and their location is of critical importance, as it facilitates engagement (figure 5.1).

In contrast with entrepreneurs, local retailers sell fewer kilograms of chapulines, and the four quartiles show a much lower range of sales. Local retailers tend to focus their energies on markets within their home

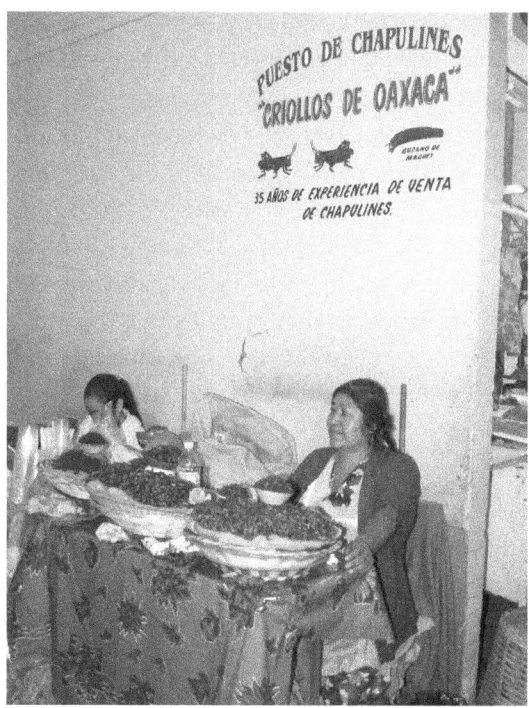

FIGURE 5.1. *An entrepreneur and third-generation chapulinera, Mercado 20 de Noviembre, Oaxaca. Photo by author.*

communities or zonal markets in Oaxaca City. About 20 percent (n = 12) of the chapulineras we interviewed were local retailers selling to customers in their home communities and to the occasional neighbor or tourist they may encounter.

The third group of chapulineras, wholesalers (17 percent, n = 9) focus their efforts on moving larger quantities of chapulines to buyers for resale. There are many reasons why chapulineras might choose wholesale work. First, they may not want to sell directly to clients, but instead enjoy working as brokers, negotiating larger orders, which tend to be more predictable and less volatile. Second, they may lack the experience, training, and connections needed to be in front of clients daily. Third, other responsibilities—including managing young children and older parents or working another job—might limit their time, making the predictability of the wholesale business necessary. While wholesalers might be expected to sell at a lower overall cost for purchases made in bulk, in the market for chapulines they often charge more per kilogram than do other vendors. Wholesalers argue that their ability to anticipate and meet demand, filling large orders quickly and with little delay, pushes up the price per kilogram for chapulines. Nevertheless, while wholesalers find steady and regular demand, they do not move as much product as entrepreneurs and local retailers.

The fourth group of chapulineras focuses their energies on meeting the needs of their immediate and extended families. Of those chapulineras we interviewed, 10 percent (n = 5) were concentrated on feeding their children and household. While these women sometimes find clients and sell when they can, they do not focus on the larger market for chapulines. The total amount of chapulines they move tends to be small, from two to fifteen kilograms daily, but more importantly, their incomes are inconsistent over time. This group sees sales to tourists as a way to earn a small bonus, beyond their daily sales.

There are also women who are hired to sell chapulines by the day. They are not chapulineras; rather, they are *ambulantes* (street vendors). *Ambulantes* are hired by wholesalers to walk the markets and surrounding areas to sell chapulines. They are paid a set wage and expected to make a given number of sales. Typically, the contracts between employer and employee are casual and part-time. Young women can move in and out of their roles as they need. These women have no set clients and have minimal background knowledge concerning chapulines.[2]

As of 2022, a kilogram (2.2 pounds) of chapulines sold for an average of MXN 350 and ranged from around MXN 300 to MXN 600. Chapulineras as a group sold an average of just under seven kilograms weekly, for an income of approximately MXN 2,450 per week.[3] Real sales ranged from a low of one or two kilograms per week among local retailers and wholesalers to a high of forty kilograms per week among the most aggressive and active entrepreneurs.

Entrepreneurs in our study charged an average of MNX 336 per kilogram, while local retailers charged about 10 percent less, or MNX 307. Wholesalers posted the highest prices for their chapulines, earning on average MNX 343 per kilogram. Chapulineras who are focused on their families and do not participate in regular sales often give their chapulines in exchange for other foods. Nevertheless, those we interviewed valued their chapulines quite highly, estimating their worth at MXN 408 per kilogram. While the cost of a kilogram of chapulines does not vary substantially by group, entrepreneurs often charge more than

Table 5.2. Who Collects Chapulines

	Self	Children	Parents	Workers	Other
entrepreneurs (n = 29)	9 (31%)	1 (3%)	1 (3%)	16 (55%)	2 (7%)
local retailers (n = 12)	6 (50%)	3 (25%)		2 (17%)	1 (8%)
wholesalers (n = 10)	4 (40%)	1 (10%)		3 (30%)	2 (20%)
family providers (n = 5)	1 (20%)	1 (20%)	1 (20%)		2 (40%)

local retailers, who sometimes give discounts to familiar, longtime clients from their home village. Wholesalers who facilitate the movement of large orders between buyer and seller earn a little more than entrepreneurs and local retailers per kilogram, but entrepreneurs sell more product in the long run. Chapulineras who earn less typically have fewer clients and use their work to supplement other income sources. Chapulineras selling ten or more kilograms of chapulines per week are typically engaged with a much larger client base and with clients who live outside of the chapulinera's home community or in Oaxaca City.

Entrepreneurs spend nearly their entire day in the marketplace meeting with clients and managing sales. They do not have time to harvest, process, and prepare chapulines on their own. In fact, entrepreneurs employ several different strategies to harvest and process chapulines for sale (see table 5.2). Nearly 30 percent of entrepreneurs put time into the harvest. They also hire others or look to family members for support. Nevertheless, around 51 percent of the crop is collected by paid workers. This contrasts with local retailers, who rely on paid workers to process about 17 percent of their harvest, and wholesalers, who employ workers to cover about 30 percent of the harvest. Chapulineras who are focused on the needs of their families harvest and process chapulines on their own or with family.

Working with hired help to harvest chapulines and having to meet large orders affects how chapulineras organize production. While some draw from their own fields, at least early in the season, alternatives include harvesting from communal fields belonging to a village, turning to neighboring milpas, and buying from distant fields (see table 5.3).

Table 5.3. Where Chapulines Are Collected

	Own/family's milpa or garden	Communal/village land	Neighbor's milpa/garden	Other source	Unknown/wouldn't say
entrepreneurs (n = 31)	19	5	4	8	14
local retailers (n = 12)	8	2		1	6
wholesalers (n = 10)	7	2		3	4
family providers (n = 6)	4	2		1	3

Buying freshly harvested and prepared chapulines is not something many people would talk about in interviews. There is an assumption that the harvest and preparation of chapulines is a family affair, built on a tradition that is thousands of years in the making. Nevertheless, many chapulineras choose to buy fresh chapulines from others, and to do otherwise would jeopardize their incomes. Chapulineras who sell ten or more kilograms of chapulines weekly can earn well, and we encountered chapulineras making as much as MXN 14,500 (around USD 700 in summer 2022), far outpacing wage expectations for rural Oaxacan women.

I learned a lot from the chapulineras we interviewed; nevertheless, my ability to understand the size of the market and its economic impact on the region was hindered by the fact that the state considers chapulines to be a pest rather than a food source and does not track production for consumption or sales. Chapulines fall under the control of the Secretaría de Agricultura y Desarrollo Rural (Secretariat of Agriculture and Rural Development), which, though cognizant of the value of chapulines as a food source, is focused on their control and eradication. One of the greatest fears for the secretariat is plague, or the infestation of crops by insects, including grasshoppers. Plagues are a regular threat to crops throughout Mexico. For example, in 2022, a plague of *Brachystola magna* (plains lubber grasshoppers), likely caused by drought, threatened the destruction of bean crops in the state of Chihuahua. The secretariat partnered with growers, other state-run agencies, and farmers to develop responses, including the use of pesticides.

Chapulineras sell more than chapulines in the marketplace (see table 5.4). Several factors influence what is for sale, including, most importantly, seasonality. Young chapulines arrive with the spring rains, as do other seasonal insects, including *chicatanas*. Many vendors, including 83 percent of the entrepreneurs interviewed for this project, also prepare the seasoning blend *sal de gusano* and sell it in small bags, alongside strings of prepared *gusanos*. The way in which chapulines are prepared and presented can also influence sales. As the season progresses, many chapulineras sell both nymphs and adult chapulines and present different flavors as well. Chapulineras describe the flavor variations as painted (*pintado*) and often include spicy chile-infused chapulines alongside more typical fare.

Across all groups, about half of the chapulineras interviewed reported selling chapulines exclusively. The rest sold some combination of *sal de gusano*, vegetables, crafts (*artesanías*), and other assorted foodstuffs and goods, such as tortillas, mole, and cheeses (typically locally made *queso fresco* or *quesillo*). Just under 12 percent of the chapulineras we interviewed (two entrepreneurs, three local retailers, and two wholesalers) reported selling vegetables—often picked up for a discount and sold as a supplement to their income from chapulines. The artful placement of produce around the chapulines creates an inviting and appetizing image of the edible insect for potential clients.

Chapulines sell quickly, but chapulineras still work hard to market their products aggressively. Whether selling from a stand, from a basket, or from the corner of the marketplace, chapulineras put energy into their presentation of chapulines. The prepared grasshoppers are piled high in large baskets, and the baskets are decorated with flowers and fresh vegetables. The stalls are clean, and the chapulines never become litter on the table. The aroma combines with the visuals to create a sense of intense, appetizing deliciousness that invites clientele.

Entrepreneurs and local retailers set up their stands and sell directly to their clients. Entrepreneurs lease stalls in the marketplace, paying a fee for the privilege of space and using it as their primary place of work. Local retailers also set up in the marketplace, but they are often not in Oaxaca City and will shift to work from home as necessary. Wholesalers tend to concentrate in the marketplace, with many working out of stalls in the Centro de Abastos.

Whether a chapulinera works from home or from the marketplace,

Table 5.4. Sales in Addition to Chapulines

	Sal de gusano	Vegetables	Crafts	Other
entrepreneurs (n = 29)	24	2	1	17
local retailers (n = 12)	7	3	1	6
wholesalers (n = 10)	3	2	1	
family (n = 6)	1			2

she is focused on her business and the need to meet demand. These efforts are transactional. Minerva García (Mercado la Merced, June 2022) summarized her situation well: "It's me, nothing else. Nothing more [gesturing to her baskets of prepared chapulines]; this here is it. My children help harvest, and we put them together, clean them up, and set them out by size. And you know, it is enough." Carla Martínez added, "I'm always here [in the market], every day, daily, I don't do anything more. When I've got to stay home, I'll send someone else. But I need to be here, yes, to sell every day, whether big or small, *chicatanas* or peanuts, I'm here all the time."

CHAPTER 6

BUILDING A TOUCHLESS ECONOMY

> When the pandemic hit, I said to myself, "Look, you need to keep selling, but from home." I know where I am, and I know my clients. I also know how much people want, how many kilos of chapulines they will buy. So people came to my house. Sometimes they would bring me their harvest; other times they would call and ask for two or three kilos. I could do that.
> —DOÑA CARMEN MENDOZA, MERCADO BENITO JUÁREZ, OAXACA, 2022

> During the pandemic, I continued to work from home, but sales went down a lot, a lot! People did not know what to do sometimes. There was always a possibility that I could make a sale, but my customers did not always know what they needed or how to contact me.
> —DOÑA FERNANDA RUIZ, MERCADO LA MERCED, OAXACA, 2022

March finds most Oaxacans anticipating the arrival of spring and the coming rainy season. It is a time to prepare fields and to look forward to a new crop of chapulines. March 2020 was not normal. Mexico was moving toward lockdown in response to the arrival of COVID-19, and it declared a nationwide health emergency on March 20 (Secretaría de Gobernación 2020). The first cases were reported in February, and the fear of an uncontrolled pandemic quickly reset expectations and left everyone scared. The federal government initiated a surveillance program, states closed public spaces including marketplaces, and schools shifted to virtual platforms. Rural communities throughout the nation sealed their entrances and organized to limit movement. At the same time, public health programs encouraged masks, handwashing, and prophylactic preventative actions (Ibarra-Nava et al. 2020).

Poor coordination of federal, state, and local programming—as well as unequal access to health care for rural and Indigenous populations, combined with the climate of uncertainty—exacerbated problems and led many people, including the chapulineras we interviewed, to worry that there were few effective ways to respond to the pandemic. In the absence of a coordinated action plan from the federal and state governments, and with little fanfare, most rural and Indigenous communities in Oaxaca reacted to the lockdown by erecting blockades to effectively isolate. The hope of many rural Oaxacan communities was that by curtailing movement and travel both into and out of villages, people would be safe and there would be fewer opportunities for the virus to be successfully transmitted. The strategy worked; infection and morbidity rates stayed low through the first wave of the pandemic.

Blocked roads and entrances meant, however, that deliveries were spotty at best and stores ran out of goods, especially fresh produce, meats, and dairy products. Children were unable to leave their hometowns, and many had to forgo attending regional education programs. This was particularly difficult for children from smaller communities that lacked programming beyond elementary instruction. Finally, access to health care, already difficult and limited in most rural and Indigenous communities, grew even more irregular, as staff for clinics became hard to find.

Despite these challenges, Oaxacans managed the first wave of the pandemic well. Rates of infection and morbidity remained low through summer 2020. The Consejo Nacional de Ciencia y Tecnología (National Council of Science and Technology), the nation's leading organization for the promotion of scientific and technological advancement and research, tracked official rates of infection and mortality, and most Indigenous communities registered no or very few cases until July 2020 (see Cohen and Mata-Sánchez 2021). Unfortunately, things were quite different by the late summer and fall, as well as through 2021 and into early 2022. Despite the fact that some infection prevention protocols were in place, the virulence of new strains of COVID-19 in the second and third waves of the pandemic drove a rapid increase in infection rates and mortality.[1] Oaxaca City did not escape the increases, and its population was challenged by rising infections, mortality, and comorbidities that compounded negative health outcomes (Venancio-Guzmán et al. 2022).

Nearly two-thirds (63 percent) of the chapulineras interviewed in June 2022 noted that they or a member of their family struggled with one or more health challenges before the pandemic. This included the 15 percent of chapulineras who had a family member dealing with type 2 diabetes and had difficulties finding competent care and accessing medications. Alcoholism was another challenge, with 7 percent of the chapulineras having at least one affected family member. They found themselves often covering the costs of addiction counseling and associated losses to their households. Another 7 percent had to support a family member dealing with hypertension. Many chapulineras, even when they had the funds to cover health-related costs, found the choice of care limited to stop-gap, short-term interventions.

Poverty, marginality, and geographic isolation challenged both access to and delivery of health care. With the pandemic raging, hard-to-find care grew even more difficult to access, and plans for mitigation and control were lacking. Limited access to affordable food and work (Pinzón-Pérez and Santos 2021), as well as poor services, drove an overwhelming skepticism among locals and further challenged well-being.

The skepticism of rural Oaxacans toward federal/outside programs is manifested in their continued poverty, the region's poor infrastructure, and a system that is mired in 1940s corporatist politics (Barraza-Lloréns et al. 2002; Flores Sanchez and Kai 2023; Nigenda et al. 1998). The risk of infection and threat of death did not change the situation for rural and Indigenous Oaxacans. Years of marginalization, maltreatment, and misrepresentation combined with conflicting news and debates over care to fuel increasing mistrust and skepticism.

The social inequalities separating rural from urban and Indigenous from mestizo amplified the discrimination that confronted chapulineras and constrained their actions, even as they focused their energies on adapting to the pandemic. The inequalities that marked rural and Indigenous life combined with the impacts of the pandemic on education, health care, mental health care, and work opportunities to undermine local planning and left most chapulineras to define their own solutions (Flores Sanchez and Kai 2023; Ibarra-Nava et al. 2021; Novak and Hernández Flores 2022).

Popular perceptions, media, and public programming played a central role in maintaining and reproducing deeply held mischaracterizations of rural and Indigenous peoples as uneducated, unprepared, lazy, and backwards (Tumbaga 2020). Locals are caricatured and parodied as naive and unable to cope with the world; meanwhile, outsiders, including teachers, doctors, and social workers who might help with the educational, physical, and mental challenges brought by the pandemic and isolation were not present (Dahal et al. 2022).

Redressing a pandemic and a history of discrimination is not easy, and the impacts of COVID-19 and the ongoing misrepresentation are tangible in the stress and uncertainty that chapulineras shared. They described the pandemic as confusing, with one vendor remarking, "Somedays I could sit in the market; other days, it was closed. I never knew what to expect or why!" (Regina Ríos, San Lorenzo, June 2022). Natalia Fuentes (Mercado la Merced, June 2022) added, "Surveillance during the pandemic, wow. There was always someone to take your temperature and check to make sure you had a mask. That was not good for sales, and we're only now feeling like it is more normal."

Some chapulineras also faced infection. Doña Catalina Herrera (Zimatlán, June 2022) shared: "When I had COVID, I stayed home and sold from my house. Everyone knew where my house was in San Pablo [Huixtepec], and they could come and get however many kilos—one or two or three kilos of chapulines. They would just call me. I didn't take anything then. I told them, 'You don't need to give me anything, later, okay?' And later I collected on the sales." Like other chapulineras, she had to adjust to a new normal defined by the pandemic and limited access. Her quick response was critical and helped her cope with the closed markets. Describing that summer, she noted that the market "dropped by half, 40 percent and then 50 percent! Now it is coming back, but it is still not the same."

Doña Catalina Herrera was not the only chapulinera to be confronted by a collapsing marketplace, pandemic, and ongoing discrimination. Daniela Aquino Díaz (Mercado Benito Juárez, June 2022) was forced out of the marketplace and began to work at home. A vendor who typically buys prepared chapulines from others to sell, she noted that the pandemic changed what she could sell: "It was not the same after the lockdown. I had to change what I was selling. I just did not have everything. I could find fresh chapulines, and we would hold them in a box at home, but it was hard to prepare enough in our kitchen. We stopped selling painted chapulines. We really only sold fresh chapulines. Everything was fresh; that was what we could do."

Chapulineras depend on a steady stream of clients for their sales. Many chapulineras have set lists of clients and connect with them face-to-face in and around their homes and the marketplace. They depend on their cell phones to connect and to finalize sales. Cell phones, though ubiquitous in the region, are still something rather new. For some they can seem disruptive, particularly when a chapulinera stops mid-discussion to take a call. However, for chapulineras, the cell phone connection facilitates their relationships and often reproduces a sense of engagement and commitment that are assumed to have been more common in past generations.

Many chapulineras inherited their clientele from their mothers and grandmothers. They assumed control of the market, and they depend on their cell phones to facilitate the transition from one generation to another. Elisa Valeriano (Mercado Benito Juárez, June 2022), a chapulinera from Santa Lucía, shared that her grandmother had taught her mother and then taught her and her sisters, and now she is "dedicated to selling grasshoppers in the same market and to many of the same people."

Cell phones can play a supporting role during interactions and in a business setting, though they can be socially disruptive and create tensions for those who lack access (Heyman and Kushlev 2023). Nevertheless, the majority of chapulineras use their cell phones to stay in contact and build long-term relationships with their clients. While these relationships are key to food and chapulines, vendors also learn about family, build friendships, and connect to new clientele, some of whom live far away and are interested in shipping chapulines across state and international borders.

Clear cell phone connections are critical when time is of the essence and a sale or delivery needs to take place quickly, or when chapulineras and clients are not physically adjacent. Bargaining and sales that might have been missed or simply impossible to conduct in the past can take place. In a similar vein, sales and deliveries can be updated, expanded, and revised in real time. Whether talking or (more often than not) texting, vendors and clients can save time, make good on contracted deliveries, and respond to any other challenge that might emerge, including a pandemic.

The flexibility of cellular service was not lost on chapulineras around the pandemic, and that flexibility extended to the chapulines market as it rebounded with an end to lockdowns, the return of tourists, and the reopening of villages. Cellular service continued to facilitate connections and business transactions as vendors and clients communicated through texts, voice calls, and video calls. The positive impact of cellular technologies extended beyond the daily needs of the market and supported chapulineras as they used the system to break out of the gender expectations that limited them.

Chapulineras, like most businesswomen throughout Mexico and much of Latin America, find that gender stereotyping, traditional gender expectations, and gender inequalities can complicate work. Gender stereotypes are further exacerbated when the businesswomen in question are rural or Indigenous. Stereotypes and expectations of businesswomen as mothers first—and as women focused on familial demands and the needs of others rather than on themselves or their business—can limit success, innovation, and entrepreneurism (Cruz-Torres 2023; García and Welter 2013). Assumed gender inequalities, particularly in rural Mexico, make it nearly impossible for women to appear as primary breadwinners, engaged participants in a global marketplace, and individuals focused on business success (Lyon et al. 2017).

In this regard, cell phones, cellular technologies, and messaging services can support chapulineras in their interactions with vendors and clients. The use of texts hides identities and can slow or stall the impact of socially assumed differences, stereotypes, and problematic expectations. In the process, chapulineras can more effectively establish themselves and their place in the market as technology demarcates the boundaries of their businesses. Furthermore, while many chapulineras are happy to work with their clients by scheduling payments, avoiding interest charges, and going out of their way to fulfill orders, cellular technologies make it easier to track down and confront a person who is trying to take advantage of the situation, not pay a bill, or abuse a family-based discount. The cell phone also becomes an effective tool for dealings with overzealous tourists, buyers, and others.

Chapulineras adapted their work to the pandemic and the uncertainty of the moment as they established new pathways to stay in contact with their clients. More than simply a loss of sales, something most were ready for, the pandemic meant a real risk of losing clients. While few voiced a fear of long-term economic ruin from the pandemic, everyone recognized that their businesses were suffering. Doña Paola noted, "There was a time when I just didn't go out. The market in Tlacolula was empty. The market in Oaxaca was closed—it was locked! The entrances to most villages, closed for year! I just didn't go out."

While the pandemic threatened to fundamentally change the market and take wealth away from locals (Gutiérrez Rodríguez 2018; van Bavel and Scheffer 2021), chapulineras regrouped and established a touchless economy. They constructed their touchless economy to shift away from closing markets amid the growing isolation. In the process, they relied on their phones to coordinate with suppliers and clientele and to limit physical contact as well as promote social distancing. The key to the touchless system was a reliance on WhatsApp, a free messaging and calling app that works across devices and platforms using end-to-end encryption to protect users' identities.

The reliance of chapulineras on their cell phones and WhatsApp grew out of Mexico's Federal Telecommunications Law in 2013 (Reguart 2021). While the cost of cell phones and phone plans is high in Mexico, the legal code revisions increased competition, investment, and consumer benefits, and opened the telecommunications market to foreign direct investment. The changes also established an independent regulatory agency as well as a public-private partnership to expand wireless broadband coverage while protecting the rights of users, including the right to clear and accurate information about their service (see Sada 2013).[2]

The reforms lowered the costs of service and made it possible for more Mexicans, including chapulineras, to afford cell phones. More affordable phones and phone plans facilitated chapulineras' ability to make purchases and take orders. Before the pandemic, while their phones were always accessible for placing orders, deliveries often happened in real time. Harvesters would drop off their raw or prepared chapulines most mornings, and chapulineras would spend time sorting and organizing for the marketplace. Increasingly affordable cellular phone service allowed chapulineras to contact harvesters in real time and in anticipation of demand.

The pandemic shifted the logistics of this process and moved everyone to virtual spaces. Chapulineras used WhatsApp and Facebook to keep their market functioning. WhatsApp was critical for several reasons. First, it allowed chapulineras to talk with one another. The virtual connections were critical, as women could send information, including notes, on sudden changes to markets. During the most difficult months (in the second and third COVID-19 waves), markets were often suddenly closed due to an outbreak or the presence of infected persons. Chapulineras kept one another apprised of events, closures, and sudden reopenings. Second, women were able to cover for one another, filling in when another chapulinera was sick or caring for family. Covering sales that might be difficult to meet for one reason or another, chapulineras also checked in on the health of others, the status of clients, and other forces that might be hard to track from home with the market closed. Third, chapulineras used WhatsApp to make sure that clients knew when chapulines were available, texting descriptions and photographs. Often these notes would include details about whether the chapulines were fresh or cooked, whether and how they were flavored, and how many kilograms were available. Perhaps the most important impact of WhatsApp was the opportunities that chapulineras found to make sales, maintain their business, and earn income necessary to purchase foods and personal protective equipment while also covering rising medical bills.

WhatsApp also proved critical as women negotiated with harvesters over chapulines. Unfortunately, two challenges hindered the harvest amid the pandemic. First, social distancing meant that suppliers were often unable to fully access fields or safely work with others, limiting collectors and their efforts. Second, the lockdown and abrupt closures of businesses throughout the valleys and state meant that once the insects were harvested, suppliers did not have access to equipment that could handle the preparation of large quantities of chapulines. And while a kilogram might be easy to prepare in a small kitchen and over a firepit, multiple kilograms of chapulines were a challenge with limited kitchen help and minimal technology.

In the end, WhatsApp was critical for chapulineras as they sought chapulines to sell and maintained contact with clients. Lacking prepared chapulines, many women turned to the sale of fresh, or raw, products. Once fresh chapulines were available, the chapulinera would text her clients. While chapulineras would inform clients of the projected costs in advance, many chapulineras gave people time to pay. Chapulineras did not rely on downloadable programs to transfer money or collect on sales virtually. Instead, they chose to wait. Virtual forms of payment are not an easy, convenient, or accessible option in Oaxaca or for most of rural Mexico, where many households lack bank accounts.[3] Clients were also struggling to make ends meet, and chapulines were an important food source, as meats and other proteins were expensive and hard to find.

For the chapulineras, the difficulty created by outstanding receipts did not involve a fear that a client might not pay what they owed. Most chapulineras know their clients well and have spent years working together. The connection often grows stronger over time, and there are small signals that indicate the strength of their bond. When it matters, a chapulinera will simply wait for payment. There is no interest, just a recognition that times can be tough. Upon payment a chapulinera will toss in an extra handful or two of chapulines, letting her clients know that she appreciates the business.

The connection of chapulinera to client is powerful, and it typically lasts generations, as daughters replace mothers and older chapulineras retire, leaving the market for their children. The virtual economy is no different, with the texts and memos that cross between suppliers, chapulineras, and clients serving as opportunities to check up on family and children, recognize important moments in time, and even help plan big events including quinceañeras, *mayordomías* (large, lavish celebrations that are founded in community engagement; see Ortega Olivares and Mora Rosales 2014), weddings, and funerals. While these events were largely on hold during the three years of the pandemic, the connections between chapulineras, their suppliers, and their clients continued, and when the pandemic eased and lockdowns were canceled, people returned to the market.

The virtual economy continues to function, even with the end of lockdowns and the return to a more normal calendar. Chapulineras rely on WhatsApp and other social media sites in ways they did not before the pandemic affected marketing. Vendors and buyers connect on Facebook, using groups like Chapulines Oaxaqueños and Chapulines en Venta to find one another. Posts include pictures and descriptions of chapulines, as well as details on preparation and price. The costs are consistent with the local market, with most chapulines valued at around

MXN 300 per kilogram in 2022–2024. While most listings are from local vendors and buyers in Oaxaca's central valleys, migrants in the United States, and people living in other parts of Mexico often post.

The pandemic emerged as a challenge. Chapulineras responded to the challenge: Using their cell phones, social media sites, and messaging programs, they defined a touchless alternative that worked. It brought them together with harvesters and clients and allowed everyone to share news about available stock and to organize sales and deliver orders.

The pandemic didn't stop the market. Chapulineras posted their stocks, and, with a text or call, a client could place an order. In response, the chapulinera prepared the order, texting the client to let them know it was ready. At that point, the client would arrive at the chapulinera's home, typically parking outside the main gate, texting their arrival. Backing away from the entrance to create social distancing, the client allowed the chapulinera to set the order down by the gate for pickup. Because a client picking up an order could leave their payment for collection, often no money changed hands.

Covering expenses was difficult for most rural Oaxacans, and very often, chapulineras tracked what they were owed, with an unwritten agreement to collect later. While chapulineras did not charge interest, they did expect full payment and would sometimes ask for it if a client was taking too long to pay. The success of chapulineras to sustain their businesses and support clients through the worst months of the pandemic is clear in the effectiveness of their touchless economy and its continued value in the lives of most chapulineras today.

The pandemic overwhelmed most chapulineras and the resources of rural and Indigenous communities. It pushed state programs and workers beyond their ability to respond and changed how rural and Indigenous Oaxacans interacted with their world. Chapulineras responded to the pandemic effectively. Their actions and the way they managed the people around them mitigated the economic impact of COVID-19 through most of the pandemic.

The end of lockdowns and the resurgence of tourism in Oaxaca, combined with a waning interest in the pandemic, coincided with the rebirth of the market for chapulines. While elements of the touchless market created during the pandemic remain, the struggle of chapulineras against a history of exclusion, social injustice, inadequate health care, and limited access to services has not really changed. Chapulineras are greeted with bias, expected to embrace gender stereotypes, and assumed to be more interested in the support of their communities and extended families than in themselves or their businesses. Chapulineras turned this narrative upside down and created a touchless economy that was based in social media connections and facilitated by messaging apps that brought together vendors, suppliers, and clients, establishing an alternative to the marketplace that continues to underpin ongoing business today.

CONCLUSIONS
WHY CHAPULINES?

What are chapulines, and should we be eating them? The question is straightforward, and the response is uncomplicated (see Bracho 2021). What are chapulines? They are toasted grasshoppers. Should we be eating them? There is no *should*; chapulines are on the table.

Should other people eat them? That is a more complicated question. Locals eat; outsiders experience. Locals eat first; outsiders ask questions and ponder: Are they safe? Edible? Contaminated with dangerous amounts of lead or pesticides? Insiders pick up a tortilla and wrap their chapulines tightly. Regardless of their willingness to sample chapulines, outsiders are not eating something they know and trust. They are sampling something that falls into the category "not food." Outsiders view them as inedible, potentially dirty, and quite possibly dangerous.

The various reactions of locals and outsiders are also complicated by the symbols they associate with eating. Locals are hungry and satisfy their craving with chapulines. Outsiders are hungry too, but they take a bite to be like the Other and to celebrate a vision of Indigeneity based on the assumption that present is past, connected by a rich historical arc that begins in the region's pre-Columbian origins.

Chapulines have been part of the diet in Oaxaca for centuries. They are a source of protein, calcium, and iron. Following the conquest, chapulines remained a critical food source. Nevertheless, the introduction of stock animals, new foods, and new ways of eating transformed chapulines from a critical choice in an environment that included only a few other proteins into a marker of Indigeneity, poverty, and marginality. The association of chapulines and entomophagy with Indigeneity, poverty, and marginality continued over the course of Mexico's development as a nation, and their consumption continues to reflect class and ethnic differences in the present.

Local, rural, and Indigenous Oaxacans welcome the arrival of chapulines in the spring. Their central place in the kitchen and at the table contrasts with the views of city folks, who are just as happy to eat them but use them as a complement to their everyday food choices. These contrasts emphasize the disparities in status, class, and wealth that continue to mark rural and Indigenous Oaxacans as limited by their traditions and unable to adapt. This divide challenges the reality of rural and Indigenous life in Oaxaca and limits the opportunity to embrace entomophagy as a norm.

While many Oaxacans enjoy chapulines for their taste and texture, others appreciate their nutritional value and the sustainability of their production. Still others, particularly outsiders, celebrate their exotic appeal and cultural, as well as spiritual, value and tend to overlook their role as a daily food source.

One reason to love chapulines does not invalidate another; however, it can limit the opportunity to appreciate how chapulines are used and why they remain important. Chapulines are central to the daily diet, and they gain special importance in times of crisis, including the recent pandemic. When stores closed and access to the marketplace was difficult, if not impossible, chapulines were an accessible protein source. The value of chapulines to visitors and outsiders who seek special experiences is equally important to our understanding. Nevertheless, the value of chapulines as an experience—and, in particular, the opportunity to eat like the ancestors—often contradicts or obscures an understanding of their importance to daily life and the ways in which chapulineras acting as producers and vendors create value and provide for their families.

Chapulines are a distinctive feature of Oaxacan cuisine, and they reflect the richness of the state's foodways. They are also a marker of identity for those who produce and consume them. For rural and Indigenous consumers, chapulines are food, and they represent a connection to land, heritage, and traditions. For chapulineras, they are a symbol of independence and market success. Outsiders approach chapulines as something different, an opportunity to learn about a unique culture. Each pathway holds value, yet the first two focus on the present, while the third homogenizes ethnic differences, emphasizes the past, and inadvertently denies the discriminatory reality of the present.

Following these pathways carries us beyond the local table to an understanding of the dynamic political economy of chapulines for local consumers as well as outsiders. They are food for most Oaxacans and an experience for outsiders. They create a story that is rooted in the past and models what might be edible in the future. Defined as food and symbol, chapulines elaborate how consumption by different groups captures and reproduces the inequalities that surround entomophagy as well as the complex social hierarchies that were established during the colonial era and continue to the present (Ayora-Diaz 2021). An appreciation of chapulines, their sale, and their consumption offers the chance to understand how chapulineras adapt their products to their own needs and to a changing marketplace, claim authority, and gain access to consumers (Jacobi et al. 2021; Moragues-Faus and Marsden 2017), whether they are rural locals, urban Oaxacans, outsiders, or Oaxacans who have migrated out of the region and settled elsewhere (Hernández Ramírez 2023).

While chapulines are more than food, their central role on the table cannot be overlooked. Their value as symbol and commodity is rooted in their status as food, their central place on the local menu, and their regular consumption. Chapulines are a model commodity, but one that can be misread if we ignore the repetitive and ritualized process of eating (Warde 2016; Wilk 2004).

Chapulineras market chapulines to earn a good living. While they confront inequality in the process, their motivations are not to correct an exploitative system. Rather, their goal is to find a viable niche in a highly unequal and exploitative system that has little space in which women, and, in particular, older, rural, and Indigenous women with limited educations, can find work and independence. Chapulineras are aware of the inequalities that define the system, and they are cognizant of just how difficult success can be. Given that reality, they are interested in maintaining a space where they can succeed, feed their families, and give their children new opportunities (see also Cruz-Torres 2023, 161).

The structural inequalities that push chapulineras, and all rural women, to the periphery of the market economy are never very far away. But a concern for success and family well-being sometimes appears to mute the critical idealism we might expect. Chapulineras are not advocating for a marketplace rethink or pushing for a training program to help them become better or richer entrepreneurs. At the same time, they are not interested in promoting entomophagy or establishing a new way of eating. They approach the market as best they can and exploit the openings they can find. They innovate when possible, as when they developed a touchless market system around the pandemic, and are always focused on securing the best price for their grasshoppers.

The practicalities of chapulines production, the selfishness that sometimes seems to pervade the approach of chapulineras to the marketplace, and their focus on business point to what is best thought of as a kind of pragmatic political economy. A pragmatic political economy of chapulines—or, more generally, of food—prioritizes practical realities and outcomes while grounding actions in their broad social, cultural, and historical contexts (Jacobi et al. 2021).

Sidney W. Mintz (1985, 4), in *Sweetness and Power*, his political history of the growth of the sugar trade and the rise of one of the first truly global commodities, argued that "what we eat, how we eat it, and how we feel about it are phenomenologically interrelated matters; together, they speak eloquently to the question of how we perceive ourselves in relation to others." Chapulines, much like sugar, are to be understood as food, as culture, and as economy. Exploring the complexity of chapulines reveals their position in ongoing contests around eating, social status, and access to power and meaning, and facilitates the sort of investigation that has "seldom been undertaken systematically" (De Garine 1979, 895).

Chapulines today are not the chapulines of the deep past; they are part of a dynamic market system that contradicts local assumptions about labor and the work of rural and Indigenous women. Following chapulineras through the marketplace makes clear how the past is baked into the structure of economic life in the present. Tracing how chapulineras respond to the marketplace and the pandemic offers an alternative way to conceive economic life. Chapulineras are inventing a new kind of entrepreneurism, one based on close ties to clients but in which the women are still most interested in making a profit and are not easy to sway.

One of the most surprising outcomes of this work is what it can tell us about development. Out-migration remains a serious challenge in Oaxaca. While the high rates of out-migration in the 1990s and early 2000s have moderated in recent years, there is still a steady flow of Oaxacans out of the state and across the border (Cohen 2004a; Vaccaro and Ortiz Díaz 2021). Chapulineras generally are not migrants. Their children and extended families are also largely defined by people who stay put.

In season, chapulines are a treat to be savored, a special dish, and a critical part of the rural Oaxacan table. Doña Miriam García's response (Zimatlán, June 2023) to the questions of why she eats chapulines, why her family eats chapulines, and why we should eat chapulines captures their importance: "My children, they grab them and fill their tacos, as many as they can! And they just start eating them, sometimes with beans, sometimes without. . . . When they are in season, they will eat chapulines every day, daily! They are always eating. . . . There is so much experience in our family, so much experience with chapulines. We share our memories, like the moment that I taught them how to harvest and how to cook."

Chapulines fill a space like Marcel Proust's (1970) madeleine. A simple cookie, the madeleine is a vehicle that, through its aroma, taste, and presence, creates involuntary memories and carries Proust, the eater, from his present to his childhood. Cloaking the negative and dulling the sharp sting of undesirable outcomes, the madeleine brings past and present together in fantasy that creates a sense of security, belonging, and care (Smith 2016).

Eating chapulines creates its own fantastic memories of the past that emphasize the positive. It is a celebration of tradition, foodways, family, and faith that lingers in blue skies, plentiful and fresh foods, warm companionship, and deep trust (Hernández Ramírez 2023). This image of chapulines does not acknowledge the role they play as a symbol of poverty or a food that is associated with social inequality. Instead, chapulines are a potent and powerful reminder of family, the love and devotion of a mother for her children, and the simplicity of rural life. Consumption establishes a through line that connects rural Oaxacans to their community and one another.

Eating chapulines is an integrative practice for locals as well as for Oaxacans living outside the state. For migrants who may be settled across international borders, chapulines are, along with tortillas and other foods, habituating (Grieshop 2007). They codify and regulate what it means to be Oaxacan and why belonging matters (Warde 2016, 121). And while anyone can make chapulines anywhere, the connection of production to rural Oaxaca is clearly important. Many chapulineras ship directly to consumers across the country and to those living across international borders. Some chapulineras physically deliver to consumers in the United States, driving to the southern border to meet buyers, who may themselves travel several days to make their purchases. For consumers who are not in Oaxaca but know Oaxaca as their ancestral homeland, chapulines smell and taste familiar. Their aroma, color, and taste are a reminder of the comal, skilled hands, an open fire, and their origins. Once more filling the space of Proust's madeleines, chapulines prepared in Oaxaca and shipped to new destinations support migrants as they settle and make their new hometowns familiar (Green et al. 2023; Soleri et al. 2023).

While eating chapulines summons nostalgia, a sense of family, and a connection to place for rural and Indigenous Oaxacans at home and for migrants living abroad, it conjures a very different world for outsiders (Hernández Ramírez 2023). For outsiders, including foodies and tourists, chapulines are a symbol that stands for connections to a distant, pre-Columbian past they can only imagine. One of a series of foods referenced as a "food of the gods," chapulines are mystical and fantastic. They are not a part of the everyday table; rather, they are a product of the deep past that has become unique in the present.

With chapulines moved off the table and out of the marketplace, their use and value in the daily lives of rural and Indigenous Oaxacans is lost, as their role is now refocused on creating an experience. In other words, chapulines are no longer a madeleine for the living; they are a symbol for outsiders and part of an imagined past. Chapulines are less a valuable protein source and more an escape from the ordinary. Eating chapulines shows that consumers have an idea of what it means to be Indigenous, and they are ready to meet the challenge of eating the inedible. Eating chapulines is a form of virtue signaling for outsiders, who highlight their acceptance of "weird" and inedible foods, their ability to embrace a challenge and try something new, and their ability to support a way of eating that holds the promise of sustainability (Pali-Schöll et al. 2019).

While celebrating the experience, outsiders' approach to chapulines diminishes its social value, making it impossible to understand why they are critical to growers, harvesters, vendors, and consumers. Growers do not practice the farming techniques that were the norm three thousand to five thousand years ago. Not only are there new crops and new ways of managing land, but also the life cycle of the grasshopper is not the same. Chapulines are concentrated on two crops in today's Oaxaca, alfalfa and *maíz*, and alfalfa was introduced to the Americas only after the conquest.

Perhaps not surprisingly, one critical concern of outsiders is whether chapulines are contaminated by heavy metals and pesticides. The fear is not unfounded, as there is a danger of lead contamination with the use of certain pottery, and there has been problematic reporting on the dangers of pesticides (see Handley et al. 2007). Nevertheless, chapulines are generally quite clean and safe to eat. Pesticides are not often a problem, both because most rural and Indigenous farmers cannot cover their high costs and because growers and chapulineras are cognizant of their changing marketplace and are planting *maíz* with the intent to feed chapulines. Rather than growing food for their own consumption, they are counting on their plots of *maíz* to support the grasshoppers.

Unfortunately, a focus on outsiders and their experience of eating chapulines means that little attention is paid to the grasshoppers' value in the local economy. The story of chapulines is not a linear one; rather, they are one of several foods that fed Oaxacans as they adapted to and coped with the conquest, colonial rule, the consolidation of the Mexican state, and, more recently, globalization, migration, and the pandemic. Nevertheless, a focus only on the experience of eating misrepresents their everyday value and use as well as the struggles and social inequalities that continue to define the lives of most chapulineras.

Chapulines are a choice, and that choice has changed through time. From one of the only protein sources available in the deep past of the region, chapulines became the choice for Indigenous Oaxacans, who were not able to partake of new proteins introduced by the Spanish. Through the many centuries of colonial rule and exploitation, chapulines were an important food source when droughts and other crises hit. In the twentieth century, chapulines, like tortillas and other foods that were defined as Indigenous, were censored and described as lacking (Denham and Gladstone 2020; Ochoa 2000).

Equally problematic is the assumption that the contemporary production of chapulines for the marketplace follows rules created in the pre-Columbian past. First, this assumption renders the actions of everyone, including chapulineras, archaic. Second, it presupposes that

FIGURE C.1. Sister chapulineras and entrepreneurs, Mercado 20 de Noviembre, Oaxaca. Photo by Andrew Mitchel.

production is organized around family and provisioning, and discounts the dynamics of the marketplace (Feinman and Nicholas 2021). Finally, it overlooks and invalidates the efforts of chapulineras as they reinvent the market and rethink the economy.

Chapulineras authored a new approach to business in response to the pandemic. The system they created for accessing, processing, and selling chapulines maintained the market through the pandemic and in the face of lockdowns and closures. Even before the arrival of COVID-19, chapulineras were transforming themselves and reimagining their roles in the market and at home. Chapulineras reject the core assumption that rural and Indigenous Mesoamerican women are defined by their roles as homemakers. They also put an end to the belief that women's work is supplemental to the efforts of husbands, fathers, and brothers. Chapulineras are businesswomen: They are not supplementing a household's income but rather acting as the primary moneymakers. They are ready to take risks and lead their families out of poverty. The burden is serious, and the commitment is sometimes overwhelming, but personal success is clear in their work, the support they can give to their children, and the ways in which their efforts can limit the pressure for other household members to migrate.

An ecologist focused on climate change would likely say that eating chapulines makes a lot of sense. We should do it to save the planet. Eating insects, insect by-products, and insect eggs and larvae is sustainable. Edible insects pack a lot of nutrition and can be turned into a myriad of tasty dishes (van Huis et al. 2013, 2022). None of that matters to Oaxacans. They eat chapulines because they are delicious.

Every chapulinera knows what to tell visitors to the region. "Gringo," they will say, "eat these insects. They are good for you. High in protein and low in fat." Who wouldn't want to try them? Chapulineras are amazing women (figure C.1). They have taken a simple bite and turned it into a valuable commodity.

Señora Reyes was one of the first chapulineras I interviewed in 2007. She described chapulines as "a gift from god" that costs almost nothing and provides so much in return. She built her business and opened her restaurant around chapulines and other wonderful dishes, including many local delicacies and even some imported specialties. But it is the chapulines she always comes back to. She doesn't sell a lot to tourists, but when she does, she serves them with a shot of mezcal to create an experience. She hopes her customers will go on to spend a lot of money in her establishment. That hope is gift enough, and it has enabled her to put her children through college, including graduate training, build a ranch, and develop her own cooking school.

ACKNOWLEDGMENTS

Several grants made this work possible. My first round of fieldwork, in 2006, was supported by the National Geographic Society. That study, "Chapulines: The Socioeconomic and Nutritional Importance of Grasshoppers in Rural Oaxaca, Mexico," allowed me to begin documenting chapulines and the chapulineras who sell them. I followed that project with two seed grants from The Ohio State University's Institute for Population Research: "The Cultural Meaning and Nutritional Value of Traditional Foods for Oaxacans in a Transnational Setting" (2006) and "An International Interdisciplinary Approach to Reducing Lead Contamination in Traditional Foods Among Mexican Migrants in the US and Communities of Origin: The Contributions of Epidemiology, Anthropology, and Community Development" (2007). In addition, support from the Fulbright–García Robles program allowed me to spend a semester teaching and in residency with the Instituto Tecnológico de Oaxaca. My home department at Ohio State has always given me the space I need to develop my research, which, in 2019, culminated in my National Science Foundation grant, "Household Producer Effects of Rural Diet Transformation" (BCS award #1918324). That project is the source of much of the data summarized here.

Of course, any grant is only as good as the people who make it shine, and I have been blessed to be surrounded by the very best. My mentor, Dr. Richard Wilk, helped me become what I am today. His curiosity, intellect, and faith in my ability continue to guide my research. My years in graduate school at Indiana University are far off, but Rick, Dennis Conway, Anya and Ron Royce, and Ray DeMallie are just a few of the people who inspired me. Ron and Ray are no longer with us, and I am sorry that they cannot read and comment, but I try my best to emulate what they taught me, both in my writing and as I mentor the next generation of anthropologists.

My students push me to be the very best, and they are central to this project. Foremost among them is Andrew Mitchel. Andrew was my field assistant in Oaxaca and directed research over two seasons in the summers of 2022 and 2023. A skilled researcher in his own right, Andrew managed to more than double the surveys and the interviews we collected, and many of the quotes in this book come from interviews he led. My thanks as well to Francisco Alejandro "Alex" Montiel Ishino, PhD. Alex earned his BA at Ohio State, and he was the first student I sent to Oaxaca to study foodways, chapulines, and well-being. He is now a research scientist at the National Institutes of Health, and we continue our collaborations. A bit later, Nidia and Nadia Merino Chavez joined me and visited Oaxaca to work with chapulineras in Zimatlán, collecting data with me on foodways and the changing diet.

Nydia Delhi Mata-Sánchez, MA, is my Oaxaca connection. A gifted scholar and field-worker, she joined me on several projects. Nydia also helped found the Universidad Tecnológico de los Valles Centrales de Oaxaca (UTVCO) and served as its *rectora* (university leader or director). She gave us a research home in Oaxaca, managed the logistics of fieldwork, and populated my field team with the best students UTVCO had, including Fernando I. Martínez Martínez, Jocelyn Osorio Feria, Paola N. Sánchez Romero, Yetlanelsi M. Santos Velasco, Miriam M. Santiago Hernández, and Erick A. Melchor Valeriano, our in-field director.

Several undergraduate anthropology majors from The Ohio State University also contributed to this project. Ember Zaahir and Mason Tolbert had their trips to Oaxaca thwarted by COVID-19 closures, but we were able to develop virtual projects that kept us occupied in some of the worst months of the pandemic. Michael Doulas joined Andrew and me in the field in 2022, and together we focused on how public space was used in the city.

No project is possible without the support of family and friends, and I remain forever in debt to Maria, my wife and partner in every project. Her patience, insights, and ability to polish my writing are a gift. Thank you also to my family, who have given me their endless support. My cousin, colleague, and friend Dr. Paulette Schuster read and reread this project, bringing her own expertise in food studies to push me to be better. Dr. Ibrahim Sirkeci, my friend and partner in the study of migration, was also integral to completing this work. He gave me a forum to start talking about chapulineras, and I thank him for listening. Thanks to Dr. Julie Lesnik, whose work on human evolution and entomophagy inspires and informs me. Drs. Steffan Igor Ayora-Diaz, Lisa Beiswenger, Ronda Brulotte, Douglas Crews, Jim Grieshop, Debbie Guatelli-Steinberg, Simos Magliveras, Scott McGraw, Bernardo Rios, Gordon Ulmer, and Ronald Waterbury listened, commented, and supported me through this work.

It was a special treat to share my research with Simon Majumdar and record an episode of his fantastic podcast *Eat My Globe*. Thank you, chef! His enthusiastic invitation to chat about entomophagy was inspirational as I completed this write-up. Give his podcast series a listen at https://www.eatmyglobe.com/.

A special thanks to Dr. Arthur Murphy. Art has been a friend and mentor since we first met in the late twentieth century (doesn't that sound dramatic). I am not sure that he realized how often I would ask for his advice; his friendship is priceless.

My greatest debt is to the chapulineras who gave of their time to complete my surveys, sat for interviews, and invited me into their market stalls and homes. What started with a taste, grew into something special because of them. Their passion, hard work, and pride inspired me to ask questions about their lives and families, the dishes they cook, and the market they have created. I am in awe of their strength and determination and honored to share their stories. I hope that this book effectively captures the tensions that define their lives as they respond to the marketplace and pressures of tourism, the competing forces of entomophagy and entomophobia, and the everyday challenges that surround their successes.

Thank you as well to my department and our amazing staff. Finally, my thanks to Casey Kittrell and his team at the University of Texas Press. I have worked with the University of Texas Press for many years, and the people there are the very best. The readers that Casey picked to review this manuscript were exceptional; they got it. They understood I was writing a different sort of ethnography, one focused on food, people, and the dynamics of the marketplace. I hope that the revisions clarify and illuminate my discussion in light of your queries and comments.

This book and the research reported within it would not have happened without the support of many people. If I missed you, please accept my apology and know that without you this project would not have happened. Any errors remain mine alone. I have designed, directed, and delivered many projects through the years; this one is the most delicious.

NOTES

Preface

1. While the title *chapulinera* is not often heard or used in the market, it is a useful identifier.

2. The post "My First-Time Eating Chapulines: What to Know" (Marcangeli, n.d.) is a good popular introduction to consuming edible insects.

Introduction. Chapulines, Food, Thought, and Economy

1. The market, located a few blocks from the Zócalo (the city's center) and across the street from the Mercado Benito Juárez, was established in the 1880s. Its name references its location on the corner of 20 de Noviembre Street and Francisco Javier Mina Avenue and commemorates the 1910 start of the Mexican Revolution (Oaxaca de Juárez, n.d.).

2. The chapulineras referenced and quoted have been given pseudonyms. Additionally, all quotes were translated from Spanish to English and edited to accurately communicate meaning, tone, and intent.

3. Chapulines contaminated with lead were found in Monterey County, California, in 2001 and 2003, after 6 percent of children and 13 percent of pregnant women showed elevated lead levels. While these elevated levels were associated with chapulines imported from Zimatlán, the origin of the contamination is unclear. We collected chapulines from sites across the central valleys and at different stages of production to test for lead and analyze for contamination at the Trace Element Research Laboratory (TERL), The Ohio State University. The four samples included (1) freshly collected, unprocessed chapulines from fields in Mitla; (2) prepared chapulines from Mitla; (3) prepared juvenile chapulines collected near Zimatlán; and (4) prepared adult chapulines collected near Zimatlán. Only the fresh, uncooked chapulines collected in Mitla were safe, at 0.04 ppm lead. The samples from Zimatlán showed elevated lead levels of 0.7 ppm for the juveniles and 0.43 ppm for the adults. The prepared sample from Mitla showed a high level of contamination, at 140 ppm (Handley et al. 2007).

4. During the 2022 field season, the exchange rate hovered around twenty Mexican pesos (MXN) to one US dollar (USD). A small bag of chapulines costs around fifty pesos.

5. Chapulines are ubiquitous in Mexico. The classic television show *El Chapulín Colorado* (1973–1979) is a Mexican comedy series created by Roberto Gómez

Bolaños in which he plays the main character, El Chapulín Colorado, and parodies the superhero genre. A second example is the band Chapulines, which combines Mexican and Caribbean musical styles (for Chapulines playlists, see Bandcamp, n.d.; Spotify, n.d.; YouTube, n.d.).

6. Social media sites and cookbooks often present the Indigenous roots of contemporary eating; these include *Oaxaca al Gusto: An Infinite Gastronomy* (Kennedy 2011) and *The Food of Oaxaca: Recipes and Stories from Mexico's Culinary Capital* (Ruiz et al. 2021).

7. The list of dare foods continues to increase with the arrival of new and unique non-Western treats from around the world. Often, these treats, whether edible insects or something else, are associated with new tour destinations and innovative approaches to cooking (see House 2019; Hwang and Choe 2020; Svanberg and Berggren 2021).

Chapter 1. Chapulineras

1. The inequalities that define economic life are rooted in a series of long-held biases that assume that rural Oaxacan women's work is supplemental to a household's earnings (Howell 1999; King 2020) and of minor value in relation to the political life within their community (Worthen 2015).

2. SADER (established in 2018) has gone through many iterations. Originally named the General Directorate of Industry (1842–1917) and, after the Mexican Revolution, titled the Ministry of Agriculture and Development (1917–1946), the agency underwent three additional restructurings between 1976 and 2018. Grasshoppers have remained a threat and have been described as plague animals throughout these changes and in response to serious periods of crop destruction.

3. Beginning in 2007 and again in 2008 and 2009, my students and field-workers visited chapulineras in Zimatlán to collect food and nutritional data. Fieldwork began again in 2022, with additional follow-up interviews in 2023. The break between fieldwork seasons was due to a few factors, including the need to secure funding and to coordinate research and programming around the COVID-19 pandemic. The pandemic in particular caused a three-year pause, during which time travel to Oaxaca was possible but the continued interruptions to the local economy made fieldwork difficult to conduct. The delay became an opportunity to develop my investigation and follow the ways in which chapulineras reinvented their market and organized a "touchless" economy that allowed them to continue selling even during the worst months of the pandemic.

4. The Sierra Mixe, home to the Mixe (an Indigenous, ethnic minority group in Mexico), is a mountainous region to the north of the central valleys (Lipp and Edmunson 2010; Pitrou 2015).

5. Access to education and educational resources continues to be limited in rural parts of Mexico. The Borgen Project notes that only 35 percent of Oaxaca's population had completed primary school as of 2020 (Carrillo 2023). While schooling remains a challenge for the chapulineras, they were, as a group, almost twice as likely to complete their primary education than other Oaxacans. Additionally, the percentage that had completed *secundaria* (which is slightly better than the state's average of 18.5 percent) is an important indicator of the efforts chapulineras make to improve themselves and create opportunities for their children.

6. The rate of diabetes reported by our respondents was under the 2021 national average of 16.9 percent (López Sánchez et al. 2022).

7. The minimum wage has increased over the last decade but remains stubbornly low (for the average monthly wages in Oaxaca from 2010 to 2023, see Statista 2024).

8. Extreme poverty is defined by the World Bank (n.d.) as living on less than USD 2.15 per day. Those living in moderate poverty can meet their basic needs but not much else and have no savings for emergencies.

Chapter 2. The Harvest and Production

1. The website Party Bugs (n.d.) notes that "the taste of insects is greatly influenced by what they eat." It describes several insects consumed in Mexico, including chapulines, noting that "grasshoppers taste like what they were fed with and what spices they are cooked with. Some of the meatier ones taste a bit like prawns."

2. A good example of innovation is captured on the website of the online store Merci Mercado (n.d.), which features recipes, news, and press information in addition to selling *chapulín*-based foods that range from mixed cheeses to milkshakes.

3. Eating with friends in Oaxaca City in 2007, I experienced a different way to enjoy chapulines. For dinner we ate *crema de chapulines* served over pork chops, a salad with a chapulines vinaigrette, and a garlic- and *chapulín*-infused butter.

Chapter 3. Chapulines on the Table

1. Just under 80 percent of the women we interviewed listed chapulines as a food normally found in a rural home.

2. An increase in obesity and diabetes is associated with the growing reliance on ready-made, ultra-processed foods, a challenge in rural Oaxaca (Barquera and Rivera 2020).

3. Rebecca Greenwald (2024) notes the tensions surrounding tourism's growth and what she describes as the "Disneylandization" of Oaxaca. The city's popularity strains services, while Indigenous stories of the past obscure the challenges faced by Oaxacans in the present.

4. Although there is no evidence that the Zapotec community rejects spicy food, Señora Muñoz insisted that they do, in contrast to people from along the coast (her home region), where "everyone wants spice."

Chapter 4. The Chapulines Experience

1. Oaxaca City was nominated for "best tourist destination in the world" and was named Mexico and Central America's Leading City Break Destination in 2020 (Silva 2024).

2. The Luxury Wanderer website notes, "If you're brave, you'll try chapulines: toasted grasshoppers. These crunchy, smoky [sic] and salty insects are a popular snack in Oaxaca. To sweeten the deal, you can have *nieve de chapulín*, which is artisanal hand-churned grasshopper ice cream" (DeMarcos 2022).

3. In "Myths, Molinillos, and Maps: Cacao in Oaxaca," Isahrai Azaria (2019) captures the mystique of chocolate: "Mayans embraced cacao so completely that they were the ones who named it *KaKaWa*, 'the food of the gods.' As Mexico's first peoples moved, interacted, warred, and negotiated, cacao was introduced to the Mixtec and Zapotec people of the Oaxaca valley."

4. FTD Travel (n.d.) describes this annual festival as follows: "Food of the Gods Festival held in Oaxaca offers travellers with the best of the country's gastronomy. This food festival is well-known all over the world and attracts tourists and certainly the food lovers. The annual festival organized in the month of October gives an insight in the regional delicacies and the significance of the city in the culinary world. Oaxaca is a gorgeous land attracting people from all parts of the world for its diverse culture and traditions and magnificent sightseeing spots. The diverse culture of Oaxaca has cultivated the food cultures of the region. The tasty and mouth watering cuisine of the region is simply a pleasure. Food of the Gods Festival in Oaxaca City is in praise of the marvellous flavours of the region."

5. Liz Weslander (2019) describes chapulines as the region's primary protein for over five thousand years.

6. Sidestepping the violence that characterized the conquest and the poverty that continues to plague the region, Isahrai Azaria (2019) quotes a local chocolatier: "The Spanish gave us pain, oppression, and cinnamon. Oaxacan chocolate must have cinnamon. So, we have to thank the Spaniards for that."

7. Visiting chapulineras is not part of a standard Oaxaca itinerary, though outsiders may meet vendors as they tour markets.

8. In the photo tour "A Walk Through the Markets of Oaxaca," the Conservatory of the Mexican Gastronomic Culture (n.d.) notes that each "corridor is a magical place that welcomes you with anafres (tortilla stoves) lit with charcoal, and from side to side there are stalls with meat for grilling: tasajo (jerky), cecina enchilada (cured meat enchilada) and tripas (tripe), as well as all kinds of legumes on the side: radishes, spring onions, nopales (prickly pears), avocados, chilis, lemons."

9. Examples of experiential programming include Oaxaca de mis Amores (n.d.), a now-defunct website that sold regional delicacies and celebrated well-documented heritage sites, craft-producing communities, and foods: "Unlock the magic of Oaxacan chapulines and elevate your culinary repertoire. Join us today and embark on a gastronomic adventure that will leave you craving more of this authentic Oaxacan delight."

Chapter 5. How to Sell Chapulines in Oaxaca

1. Vendors from Puebla were difficult to engage. Their stands are often on the periphery of the marketplace to avoid fees. With verbal consent, we watched one vendor as she interacted with clients. Her sales were typically multiple kilos. When a restauranteur asked for a bulk discount, she laughed him off. He argued that she would be sorry, but she would have none of it, and she commented to us that she did not lack for sales.

2. It was difficult to engage with *ambulantes*. These young women needed to make minimum sales, and talking with my team only made it harder for them to reach their expected totals.

3. The Mexican federal government estimated the standard income for work in Oaxaca's informal economy during the summer of 2022 at approximately MXN 2,660 per month (Gobierno de México, n.d.).

Chapter 6. Building a Touchless Economy

1. Only eleven COVID-19 cases were identified in Indigenous communities in Oaxaca by April 2020. One year later, that number had risen to 12,873 cases. It

continued to increase through April 2022, reaching 32,411 cases. The mortality rate also rose, and Indigenous Mexicans were at a 68 percent higher risk of mortality than non-Indigenous Mexicans (Dahal et al. 2022; Gobierno de México 2023).

2. The Federal Law on the Protection of Personal Data Held by Private Parties (2012) addressed the collection, use, and storage of personal data by private entities to prevent unauthorized access and misuse.

3. About 40 percent of rural Mexican households had access to financial services in 2018 (INEGI 2018).

REFERENCES

Abril, S., M. Pinzón, M. Hernández-Carrión, and A. D. P. Sánchez-Camargo. 2022. "Edible Insects in Latin America: A Sustainable Alternative for Our Food Security." *Frontiers in Nutrition* 9:904812.

Aguilar-Støen, M., S. R. Moe, and S. L. Camargo-Ricalde. 2009. "Home Gardens Sustain Crop Diversity and Improve Farm Resilience in Candelaria Loxicha, Oaxaca, Mexico." *Human Ecology* 37:55–77.

Ahamed-Broadhurst, K. n.d. "Mexico City: Eating Like Our Ancestors." *GoNomad*. Accessed May 1, 2024. https://www.gonomad.com/121247-mexico.

Aigbedion-Atalor, P. O., K. O. Fening, A. O. Adeyemi, et al. 2024. "Regenerative Edible Insects for Food, Feed, and Sustainable Livelihoods in Nigeria: Consumption, Potential and Prospects." *Future Foods* 9:100309.

Alaniz, L. 2011. "Chapulines—An Ancestral Tradition in Oaxaca." *Leticia Alaniz* (blog), May 17. https://leticiaalaniz.blogspot.com/2011/05/chapulines-ancestral-tradition-in.html.

Alt, K. W., A. Al-Ahmad, and J. P. Woelber. 2022. "Nutrition and Health in Human Evolution—Past to Present." *Nutrients* 14 (17): 3594.

Amorós, J. E., L. Martínez Ramírez, L. Rodríguez-Aceves, and L. E. Ruiz. 2021. "Revisiting Poverty and Entrepreneurship in Developing Countries." *Journal of Developmental Entrepreneurship* 26 (2): 2150008.

Arellanes Cancino, N., and A. Sosa Perdomo. 2019. "Una comparativa entre la flora de los huertos familiares de los Estados de Oaxaca y Michoacán, México, a partir de los conocimientos tradicionales." *Arnaldoa* 26:1153–1164.

Arellano-Plaza, M., J. B. Paez-Lerma, N. O. Soto-Cruz, M. R. Kirchmayr, and A. Gschaedler Mathis. 2022. "Mezcal Production in Mexico: Between Tradition and Commercial Exploitation." *Frontiers in Sustainable Food Systems* 6:832532.

Armelagos, G. J. 2014. "Brain Evolution, the Determinates of Food Choice, and the Omnivore's Dilemma." *Critical Reviews in Food Science and Nutrition* 54 (10): 1330–1341.

Armendariz, M., C. Pérez-Ferrer, A. Basto-Abreu, G. S. Lovasi, U. Bilal, and T. Barrientos-Gutiérrez. 2022. "Changes in the Retail Food Environment in Mexican Cities and Their Association with Blood Pressure Outcomes." *International Journal of Environmental Research and Public Health* 19 (3): 1353.

Atal, J. P., H. R. Ñopo, and N. Winder. 2009. "New Century, Old Disparities: Gender and Ethnic Wage Gaps in Latin America." IDB Working Paper. Inter-American Development Bank. https://doi.org/10.18235/0010742.

Ayieko, I. A., M. Onyango, R. T. Ngadze, and M. A. Ayieko. 2021. "Edible Insects as New Food Frontier in the Hospitality Industry." *Frontiers in Sustainable Food Systems* 5:693990.

Ayora-Diaz, S. I., ed. 2015. *Cooking Technology: Transformations in Culinary Practice in Mexico and Latin America*. Bloomsbury.

Ayora-Diaz, S. I. 2021. "Nostalgia, nacionalismo, y colonialismo cultural: Las crónicas del taco." *Encartes* 4 (7): 383–390.

Azaria, I. 2019. "Myths, Molinillos, and Maps: Cacao in Oaxaca." *Qué Pasa Oaxaca*, January 26. https://www.quepasaoaxaca.com/mitos-molinillos.

Baldomero Quintana, L., L. G. Woo-Mora, and E. De la Rosa-Ramos. 2023. "Infrastructures of Race? Colonial Indigenous Segregation and Contemporary Land Values." SSRN. Last revised April 6, 2023. https://ssrn.com/abstract=4125065.

Bandcamp. n.d. "'Bululú' by Chapulines." Accessed June 10, 2024. https://chapulines.bandcamp.com/album/bulul.

Barquera, S., and J. A. Rivera. 2020. "Obesity in Mexico: Rapid Epidemiological Transition and Food Industry Interference in Health Policies." *Lancet Diabetes Endocrinology* 8 (9): 746–747.

Barraza-Lloréns, M., S. Bertozzi, E. González-Pier, and J. P. Gutiérrez. 2002. "Addressing Inequity in Health and Health Care in Mexico." *Health Affairs* 21 (3): 47–56.

Barrera-Fernández, D., and M. Hernández-Escampa. 2017. "From Cultural to Creative Tourism: Urban and Social Perspectives from Oaxaca, México." *Revista de Turismo Contemporáneo* 5:3–20.

Barrientos-Lozano, L., and P. Almaguer-Sierra. 2006. "Manejo Sustentable de Chapulines (Ortoptera: Acridoidea) en México." *Vedalia* 13:51–56.

Berdan, F. F. 1993. "Trauma and Transition in Sixteenth Century Central Mexico." In *The Meeting of Two Worlds: Europe and the Americas 1492–1650*, edited by W. Bray. British Academy.

Berger, S., C. Bärtsch, C. Schmidt, F. Christandl, and A. M. Wyss. 2018. "When Utilitarian Claims Backfire: Advertising Content and the Uptake of Insects as Food." *Frontiers in Nutrition* 5:88.

Bérubé, É., and J. E. Forde. 2024. "Oaxacan Cuisine at Achiutla during the Early Colonial Period: A Story of Resilience." In *Mesquite Pods to Mezcal: 10,000 Years of Oaxacan Cuisines*, edited by V. Pérez Rodríguez, S. Morell-Hart, and S. M. King. University of Texas Press.

Boesveldt, S., and V. Parma. 2021. "The Importance of the Olfactory System in Human Well-Being, Through Nutrition and Social Behavior." *Cell Tissue Research* 383 (1): 559–567.

Bracho, R. 2021. "What Are Chapulines." Expat Insurance, August 8. https://www.expatinsurance.com/articles/what-are-chapulines.

Brillat-Savarin, J. A. 1999. *The Physiology of Taste, or Meditations on Transcendental Gastronomy*. Translated by M. F. K. Fisher. Counterpoint Press.

Briseño-Maas, M. L., and E. Bautista-Martínez. 2016. "Violence Towards Women in Oaxaca: On the Paths of Inequality and Poverty." *LiminaR* 14 (2): 15–27.

Brulotte, R. L., and A. Starkman. 2016. "Caldo De Piedra and Claiming Pre-Hispanic Cuisine as Cultural Heritage." In *Edible Identities: Food as Cultural Heritage*, edited by M. A. Di Giovine and R. L. Brulotte. Ashgate.
Butzer, K. W. 1988. "Cattle and Sheep from Old to New Spain: Historical Antecedents." *Annals of the Association of American Geographers* 78 (1): 29–56.
Canedo, A. 2019. "Labor Market Discrimination Against Indigenous Peoples in Mexico: A Decomposition Analysis of Wage Differentials." *Iberoamericana—Nordic Journal of Latin American and Caribbean Studies* 48 (1): 12–27.
Carrillo, M. 2023. "Literacy and Education in Oaxaca, Mexico." Borgen Project, April 12. https://borgenproject.org/education-in-oaxaca/.
Castañeda Garza, D. 2024. "Moderate Opulence: The Evolution of Wealth Inequality in Mexico in Its First Century of Independence." *Explorations in Economic History* 92:101567.
Castañón, A. 2021. "The Evolution of Mexican Cuisine: Five Gastronomical Seasons, Mole, Pozole, Tamal, Tortilla, and Chile Relleno." In *Food, Texts, and Cultures in Latin America and Spain*, edited by R. Climent-Espino and A. M. Gómez-Bravo. Vanderbilt University Press.
Cerritos, R., and Z. Cano-Santana. 2008. "Harvesting Grasshoppers *Sphenarium purpurascens* in Mexico for Human Consumption: A Comparison with Insecticidal Control for Managing Pest Outbreaks." *Crop Protection* 27 (3–5): 473–480.
Cerritos-Flores, R., R. Ponce-Reyes, and F. Rojas-García. 2015. "Exploiting a Pest Insect Species *Sphenarium purpurascens* for Human Consumption: Ecological, Social, and Economic Repercussions." *Journal of Insects as Food and Feed* 1:75–84.
Choe, J., and P. Lugosi. 2023. *Migration, Tourism and Social Sustainability*. Routledge.
Cohen, J. H. 1999. *Cooperation and Community: Economy and Society in Oaxaca*. University of Texas Press.
Cohen, J. H. 2001. "Transnational Migration in Rural Oaxaca, Mexico: Dependency, Development, and the Household." *American Anthropologist* 103 (4): 954–967.
Cohen, J. H. 2004a. "Community, Economy and Social Change in Oaxaca, Mexico: Rural Life and Cooperative Logic in the Global Economy." In *Mexico in Transition: Neoliberal Globalism, the State and Civil Society*, edited by G. Otero. Zed Books.
Cohen, J. H. 2004b. *The Culture of Migration in Southern Mexico*. University of Texas Press.
Cohen, J. H., B. Everett, A. Polsky, and F. Montiel-Ishino. 2009. "Gender, Work, and Opportunity in Oaxaca: Some Thoughts on the Importance of Women in the Economic Life of the Rural Village." In *Economic Development, Integration, and Morality in Asia and the Americas*, edited by D. Wood. Emerald Group.
Cohen, J. H., and N. D. Mata-Sánchez 2021. "Challenges, Inequalities and COVID-19: Examples from Indigenous Oaxaca, Mexico." *Global Public Health* 16 (4): 639–649.
Cohen, J. H., N. D. Mata-Sánchez, and F. A. Montiel-Ishino. 2009. "Chapulines and Food Choices in Rural Oaxaca." *Gastronomica* 9 (1): 61–65.

Cohen, J. H., and L. Rodriguez. 2005. "Remittance Outcomes in Rural Oaxaca, Mexico: Challenges, Options and Opportunities for Migrant Households." *Population, Space and Place* 11 (1): 49–63.

Cohen, J. H., and P. K. Schuster. 2019. "To Eat Chapulines in Oaxaca, Mexico: One Food, Many Flavors." In *Taste, Politics, and Identities in Mexican Food*, edited by S. I. Ayora-Diaz. Bloomsbury Books.

CONAPO (Consejo Nacional de Población). 2023. *Índices de marginación por entidad federativa y municipio 2020*. Secretaría de Gobernación.

Conservatory of the Mexican Gastronomic Culture. n.d. "A Walk Through the Markets of Oaxaca." Accessed November 15, 2023. https://artsandculture.google.com/story/a-walk-through-the-markets-of-oaxaca-conservatory-of-the-mexican-gastronomic-culture/kQWROmseIR9NpA.

Cook, I., and P. Crang. 1996. "The World on a Plate: Culinary Culture, Displacement and Geographical Knowledges." *Journal of Material Culture* 1 (2): 131–153.

Cruz-Torres, M. L. 2012. "Contested Livelihoods: 'Gender, Fisheries, and Resistance in Northwestern Mexico.'" In *Gender and Sustainability: Lessons from Asia and Latin America*, edited by M. L. Cruz-Torres and P. McElwee. University of Arizona Press.

Cruz-Torres, M. L. 2023. *Pink Gold: Women, Shrimp, and Work in Mexico*. University of Texas Press.

Dahal, S., S. E. Mamelund, R. Luo, L. Sattenspiel, S. Self-Brown, and G. Chowell. 2022. "Investigating COVID-19 Transmission and Mortality Differences Between Indigenous and Non-Indigenous Populations in Mexico." *International Journal of Infectious Diseases* 122:910–920.

Dakhel, W. H., S. T. Jaronski, and S. Schell. 2020. "Control of Pest Grasshoppers in North America." *Insects* 11 (9): 566.

Danielson, M. S., and T. A. Eisenstadt. 2009. "Walking Together, but in Which Direction? Gender Discrimination and Multicultural Practices in Oaxaca, Mexico." *Politics and Gender* 5 (2): 153–184.

De Garine, I. 1979. "Anthropology of Food." *Social Science Information* 18 (6): 895–897.

DeMarcos, J. 2022. "Why You Should Visit Oaxaca City: A Foodie's Dream in Mexico." Luxury Wanderer, December 13. https://theluxurywanderer.com/destinations/why-you-should-visit-oaxaca-city-a-foodies-dream-in-mexico/.

Denham, D., and F. Gladstone. 2020. "Making Sense of Food System Transformation in Mexico." *Geoforum* 115:67–80.

De Souza, R. T. 2019. *Feeding the Other: Whiteness, Privilege, and Neoliberal Stigma in Food Pantries*. MIT Press.

Di Giovine, M. A., and R. L. Brulotte, eds. 2016. *Edible Identities: Food as Cultural Heritage*. Ashgate.

Earle, R. 2010. "'If You Eat Their Food . . .': Diets and Bodies in Early Colonial Spanish America." *American Historical Review* 115 (3): 688–713.

Earle, R. 2016. "The Pleasures of Taxonomy: Casta Paintings, Classification, and Colonialism." *William and Mary Quarterly* 73 (3): 427–466.

Endfield, G. H. 2012. "The Resilience and Adaptive Capacity of Social-Environmental Systems in Colonial Mexico." *Proceedings of the National Academy of Sciences* 109 (10): 3676–3681.

Endfield, G. H., I. F. Tejedo, and S. L. O'Hara. 2004. "Drought and Disputes, Deluge and Dearth: Climatic Variability and Human Response in Colonial Oaxaca, Mexico." *Journal of Historical Geography* 30 (2): 249–276.

Escalante-Aburto, A., L. Rodríguez-Sifuentes, C. Ozuna, et al. 2022. "Consumer Perception of Insects as Food: Mexico as an Example of the Importance of Studying Socio-Economic and Geographical Differences for Decision-Making in Food Development." *International Journal of Food Science and Technology* 57 (10): 6306–6316.

Estévez-Moreno, L. X., and G. C. Miranda-de la Lama. 2022. "Meat Consumption and Consumer Attitudes in México: Can Persistence Lead to Change?" *Meat Science* 193:108943.

Everett, B. A. 2004. "Filling the Gap: The Economic, Culinary, and Cultural Significance of Oaxacan Kitchen Gardens." Honors thesis, Pennsylvania State University.

Familar, J. 2017. "What I Learned from Women Entrepreneurs in Oaxaca." *World Bank Blogs*. World Bank, July 10. https://blogs.worldbank.org/en/latinamerica/what-i-learned-women-entrepreneurs-oaxaca.

Feinman, G. M., and L. M. Nicholas. 2021. "Marketplaces and Market Exchanges in the Pre-Colonial Americas." In *Markets and Exchanges in Pre-Modern and Traditional Societies*, edited by J. C. M. García. Oxbow Books.

Ficek, R. E. 2019. "Cattle, Capital, Colonization: Tracking Creatures of the Anthropocene in and out of Human Projects." *Current Anthropology* 60 (S20): S260–S271.

Flores Sanchez, J. M., and J. Kai. 2023. "Coloniality and Contagion: COVID-19 and the Disposability of Women of Color in Feminized Labor Sectors." *Gender, Work and Organization* 30 (2): 373–390.

Forte, M. C. n.d. "The Problem of Progressivism." The Zero Anthropology Project. Accessed November 30, 2024. http://openanthropology.org/progressivism.htm.

Friedensohn, D. 2001. "Chapulines, Mole, and Pozole: Mexican Cuisines and the Gringa Imagination." In *Pilaf, Pozole, and Pad Thai: American Women and Ethnic Food*, edited by S. Inness. University of Massachusetts Press.

FTD Travel. n.d. "Food of Gods Festival, Mexico." Accessed October 15, 2024. https://www.ftd.travel/food-of-gods-festival-attraction-mexico.

Gahukar, R. T. 2011. "Entomophagy and Human Food Security." *International Journal of Tropical Insect Science* 31 (3): 129–144.

Gallardo-López, F., A. Rendón-Martínez, G. Ramírez-Sandoval, C. Ozuna, I. Paniagua-Martínez, and A. Ramírez-Martínez. 2023. "Consumption of *Atta mexicana* (Chicatanas) in Two Regions of Veracruz, Mexico—a Multifactorial Study of the Consumption of Chicatanas." *Journal of Insects as Food and Feed* 9 (4): 525–539.

Gálvez, A. 2018. *Eating NAFTA: Trade, Food Policies, and the Destruction of Mexico*. University of California Press.

Gamlin, J. B. 2020. "'You See, We Women, We Can't Talk, We Can't Have an Opinion . . .': The Coloniality of Gender and Childbirth Practices in Indigenous Wixárika Families." *Social Science and Medicine* 252:112912.

García, M. C. D., and F. Welter. 2013. "Gender Identities and Practices: Interpreting Women Entrepreneurs' Narratives." *International Small Business Journal* 31 (4): 384–404.

García-Gaytán, V., F. C. Gómez-Merino, L. I. Trejo-Téllez, G. A. Baca-Castillo, and S. García-Morales. 2017. "The Chilhuacle Chili (*Capsicum annuum* L.) in Mexico: Description of the Variety, Its Cultivation, and Uses." *International Journal of Agronomy* 2017:5641680.

Gladstone, F. J. 2023. "Food Security and Knowledge Politics in Rural Oaxaca." *Gender, Place and Culture* 31 (6): 794–816.

Gobierno de México. 2023. "Información General." COVID-19 México, updated June 26. https://datos.covid-19.conacyt.mx.

Gobierno de México. n.d. "Oaxaca." Data México. Accessed November 4, 2023. https://www.economia.gob.mx/datamexico/en/profile/geo/oaxaca-oa.

Goertzen, C. 2010. *Made in Mexico: Tradition, Tourism, and Political Ferment in Oaxaca*. University Press of Mississippi.

Gómez Sal, A., A. González-García, and H. Doña. 2014. "La cultura del patio como soporte de agricultura familiar en América tropical." *Ambienta* 107:74–85.

Green, J. D., C. A. Reid, M. A. Kneuer, and M. V. Hedgebeth. 2023. "The Proust Effect: Scents, Food, and Nostalgia." *Current Opinion in Psychology* 50:101562.

Greenwald, R. 2024. "Amid Tourism Surge, Oaxaca Residents Resist 'Disneylandization.'" *Bloomberg*, April 10. https://www.bloomberg.com/news/features/2024-04-10/in-oaxaca-some-residents-are-fighting-back-against-gentrification.

Gregorio, S. 2021. "Taste and Taxonomy of Native Food in Hispanic America, 1492–1640." In *Food, Texts, and Cultures in Latin America and Spain*, edited by R. Climent-Espino and A. M. Gómez-Bravo. Vanderbilt University Press.

Grieshop, J. I. 2007. "The Envios of San Pablo Huixtepec, Oaxaca: Food, Home, and Transnationalism." *Human Organization* 65 (4): 400–406.

Gross, T. 2011. "Divided over Tourism: Zapotec Responses to Mexico's 'Magical Villages Program.'" *Anthropological Notebooks: Slovene Anthropological Society* 17 (3): 51–71.

Guiné, R. P. F., P. Correia, C. Coelho, and C. A. Costa. 2021. "The Role of Edible Insects to Mitigate Challenges for Sustainability." *Open Agriculture* 6 (1): 24–36.

Gullette, Gregory S. 2007. "Migration and Tourism Development in Huatulco, Oaxaca." *Current Anthropology* 48 (4): 603–611.

Gutiérrez Rodríguez, E. 2018. "The Coloniality of Migration and the 'Refugee Crisis': On the Asylum-Migration Nexus, the Transatlantic White European Settler Colonialism-Migration and Racial Capitalism." *Refuge: Canada's Journal on Refugees* 34 (10): 16–28.

Gutiérrez-Zamora, V. 2021. "The Coloniality of Neoliberal Biopolitics: Mainstreaming Gender in Community Forestry in Oaxaca, Mexico." *Geoforum* 126:139–149.

Gyimóthy, S., and R. J. Mykletun. 2009. "Scary Food: Commodifying Culinary Heritage as Meal Adventures in Tourism." *Journal of Vacation Marketing* 15 (3): 259–273.

Haley, S. D., and C. Fukuda. 2014. *Day of the Dead: When Two Worlds Meet in Oaxaca*. Berghahn Books.

Hamerman, E. J. 2016. "Cooking and Disgust Sensitivity Influence Preference for Attending Insect-Based Food Events." *Appetite* 96:319–326.

Handley, M. A., C. Hall, E. Sanford, et al. 2007. "Globalization, Binational Communities, and Imported Food Risks: Results of an Outbreak Investigation of Lead

Poisoning in Monterey County, California." *American Journal of Public Health* 97 (5): 900–906.

Hepp, G. 2019. "La política patrimonial y la diversidad cultural abreviada: Cómo el pasado y el presente de Oaxaca se han simplificado para el consumo global." *Ark Magazine* 28:28–43.

Hernández Ramírez, J. C. 2023. "Consumer Reasons for Eating Chapulines (*Sphenarium purpurascens*) in the Sierra Sur of Oaxaca." *Journal of Insects as Food and Feed* 9 (2): 213–223.

Hernández Ramírez, J. C., T. E. Almaraz, and S. M. López. 2021. "Between Rupture and Continuity: Millennials' Reasons for Eating Chapulines in the Southern Sierra of Oaxaca." *Food, Culture and Society* 25 (3): 468–487.

Hernández-Rojas, R. D., and N. Huete Alcocer. 2021. "The Role of Traditional Restaurants in Tourist Destination Loyalty." *PLOS One* 16 (6): e0253088.

Heyman, J. L., and K. Kushlev. 2023. "Did Smartphones Enhance or Diminish Well-Being During the COVID-19 Pandemic?" *Frontiers in Psychology* 14:1094196.

House, J. 2019. "Insects Are Not 'the New Sushi': Theories of Practice and the Acceptance of Novel Foods." *Social and Cultural Geography* 20 (9): 1285–1306.

Howell, J. 1999. "Expanding Women's Roles in Southern Mexico: Educated, Employed Oaxaqueñas." *Journal of Anthropological Research* 55 (1): 99–127.

Hurd, K. J., S. Shertukde, T. Toia, et al. 2019. "The Cultural Importance of Edible Insects in Oaxaca, Mexico." *Annals of the Entomological Society of America* 112 (6): 552–559.

Hwang, J., H. Kim, and J. Y. Choe. 2020. "The Role of Eco-Friendly Edible Insect Restaurants in the Field of Sustainable Tourism." *International Journal of Environmental Research and Public Health* 17 (11): 4064.

Hwang, J., and J. Y. Choe. 2020. "How to Enhance the Image of Edible Insect Restaurants: Focusing on Perceived Risk Theory." *International Journal of Hospitality Management* 87:102464.

Ibarra, J. T., A. Barreau, C. Del Campo, C. I. Camacho, G. J. Martin, and S. R. McCandless. 2011. "When Formal and Market-Based Conservation Mechanisms Disrupt Food Sovereignty: Impacts of Community Conservation and Payments for Environmental Services on an Indigenous Community of Oaxaca, Mexico." *International Forestry Review* 13 (3): 318–337.

Ibarra-Nava, I., J. A. Cardenas-de la Garza, R. E. Ruiz-Lozano, and R. G. Salazar-Montalvo. 2020. "Mexico and the COVID-19 Response." *Disaster Medicine and Public Health Preparation* 14 (4): e17–e18.

Ibarra-Nava, I., K. Flores, V. Ruiz-Herrera, et al. 2021. "Ethnic Disparities in COVID-19 Mortality in Mexico: A Cross-Sectional Study Based on National Data." *PLOS One* 16 (3): e0239168.

Imathiu, S. 2020. "Benefits and Food Safety Concerns Associated with Consumption of Edible Insects." *NFS Journal* 18:1–11.

INEGI (Instituto Nacional de Estadística y Geografía). 2018. "Encuesta Nacional de Inclusión Financiera 2018: Presentación de resultados." https://www.inegi.org.mx/contenidos/programas/enif/2018/doc/enif_2018_resultados.pdf.

Ítaka, M. 2021. "Building Blocks: Chapulines, a Bug's Culinary Life in Oaxaca." *Culinary Backstreets*, February 26. https://culinarybackstreets.com/cities-category/oaxaca/2021/chapulines-oaxaca/.

Jacobi, J., G. V. Villavicencio Valdez, and K. Benabderrazik. 2021. "Towards Political Ecologies of Food." *Nature Food* 2 (110): 835–837.
Karver, T. S., A. Sorhaindo, K. S. Wilson, and X. Contreras. 2016. "Exploring Intergenerational Changes in Perceptions of Gender Roles and Sexuality Among Indigenous Women in Oaxaca." *Culture, Health and Sexuality* 18 (8): 845–859.
Kennedy, D. 2011. *Oaxaca al Gusto: An Infinite Gastronomy*. University of Texas Press.
King, H. B. 2020. "Whose Work Is Real Work? A Triple Labor Framework for Sustainable Development Initiatives." *Economic Anthropology* 7 (2): 215–227.
King, S. M., and S. Morell-Hart. 2024. "Preserving Oaxacan Foodways in the Face of Conquest: A Seed Bank in the Nejapan Sierra Sur." In *Mesquite Pods to Mezcal: 10,000 Years of Oaxacan Cuisines*, edited by V. Pérez Rodríguez, S. Morell-Hart, and S. M. King. University of Texas Press.
Kosonen, H. 2022. "The Yuck Factor Reiterating Insect-Eating (and Otherness) Through Disgust." In *Cultural Approaches to Disgust and the Visceral*, edited by M. Ryynänen, H. Kosonen, and S. Ylönen. Routledge.
La Barbera, F., F. Verneau, M. Amato, and K. Grunert. 2018. "Understanding Westerners' Disgust for the Eating of Insects: The Role of Food Neophobia and Implicit Associations." *Food Quality and Preference* 64:120–125.
Le, D., N. Scott, and G. Lohmann. 2019. "Applying Experiential Marketing in Selling Tourism Dreams." *Journal of Travel and Tourism Marketing* 36 (2): 220–235.
Le, H. T., I. D. Brouwer, C. A. de Wolf, L. van der Heijden, K. C. Nguyen, and F. J. Kok. 2007. "Suitability of Instant Noodles for Iron Fortification to Combat Iron-Deficiency Anemia Among Primary Schoolchildren in Rural Vietnam." *Food and Nutrition Bulletin* 28 (3): 291–298.
Legendre, T. S., and M. A. Baker. 2021. "The Gateway Bug to Edible Insect Consumption: Interactions Between Message Framing, Celebrity Endorsement and Online Social Support." *International Journal of Contemporary Hospitality Management* 33 (5): 1810–1829.
Lesnik, J. J. 2018. *Edible Insects and Human Evolution*. University Press of Florida.
Lesnik, J. J. 2019. "The Colonial/Imperial History of Insect Food Avoidance in the United States." *Annals of the Entomological Society of America* 112 (6): 560–565.
Levine, M. N., and K. Puseman. 2024. "Foregrounding Food: Mixtec Cuisine, Identity and Ritual at Tututepec, Oaxaca." In *Mesquite Pods to Mezcal: 10,000 Years of Oaxacan Cuisines*, edited by V. Pérez Rodríguez, S. Morell-Hart, and S. M. King. University of Texas Press.
Lévi-Strauss, C. 1963. *Totemism*. Beacon Press.
Liceaga, A. M. 2022. "Edible Insects, a Valuable Protein Source from Ancient to Modern Times." *Advances in Food Nutrition Research* 101:129–152.
Liem, D. G., and J. A. Mennella. 2002. "Sweet and Sour Preferences During Childhood: Role of Early Experiences." *Developmental Psychobiology* 41 (4): 388–395.
Lipp, F. J., and M. S. Edmunson. 2010. *The Mixe of Oaxaca: Religion, Ritual, and Healing*. University of Texas Press.
Lira, M. G., J. P. Robson, and D. J. Klooster. 2022. "Commons, Global Markets and Small-Scale Family Enterprises: The Case of Mezcal Production in Oaxaca, Mexico." *Agriculture and Human Values* 39:937–952.
Locher, J. L., W. C. Yoels, D. Maurer, and J. van Ells. 2005. "Comfort Foods: An Exploratory Journey into the Social and Emotional Significance of Food." *Food and Foodways* 13 (4): 273–297.

López Sánchez, G. F., R. López-Bueno, C. Villaseñor-Mora, and S. Pardhan. 2022. "Comparison of Diabetes Mellitus Risk Factors in Mexico in 2003 and 2014." *Frontiers in Nutrition* 9:894904.
Lyon, S., T. Mutersbaugh, and H. Worthen. 2017. "The Triple Burden: The Impact of Time Poverty on Women's Participation in Coffee Producer Organizational Governance in Mexico." *Agriculture and Human Values* 34:317–331.
MacClancy, J. M., C. J. K. Henry, and H. Macbeth. 2009. *Consuming the Inedible: Neglected Dimensions of Food Choice*. Berghahn Books.
Magaña, V., J. A. Amador, and S. Medina. 1999. "The Midsummer Drought over Mexico and Central America." *Journal of Climate* 12 (6): 1577–1588.
Magara, H. J. O., S. Niassy, M. A. Ayieko, et al. 2020. "Edible Crickets (Orthoptera) Around the World: Distribution, Nutritional Value, and Other Benefits—A Review." *Frontiers in Nutrition* 7:537915.
Manzanero-Medina, G. I., M. A. Vásquez-Dávila, H. Lustre-Sánchez, and A. Pérez-Herrera. 2020. "Ethnobotany of Food Plants (Quelites) Sold in Two Traditional Markets of Oaxaca, Mexico." *South African Journal of Botany* 130:215–223.
Marcangeli, Sveva. n.d. "My First-Time Eating Chapulines: What to Know." Svadore. Accessed November 1, 2023. https://www.svadore.com/my-first-time-eating-chapulines-what-to-know/.
Marrón-Ponce, J. A., L. Tolentino-Mayo, F. M. Hernández, and C. Batis. 2019. "Trends in Ultra-Processed Food Purchases from 1984 to 2016 in Mexican Households." *Nutrients* 11 (1): 45.
Martin, P. M., and N. Carvajal. 2016. "Feminicide as 'Act' and 'Process': A Geography of Gendered Violence in Oaxaca." *Gender, Place and Culture* 23 (7): 989–1002.
Martínez-Martínez, O. A., K. Gil-Vasquez, and M. B. Romero-González. 2023. "Food Insecurity and Levels of Marginalization: Food Accessibility, Consumption and Concern in Mexico." *International Journal for Equity in Health* 22 (1): 178.
Martínez-Martínez, O. A., and A. Rodríguez-Brito. 2020. "Vulnerability in Health and Social Capital: A Qualitative Analysis by Levels of Marginalization in Mexico." *International Journal for Equity in Health* 19 (1): 24.
Marx, K. (1867) 1992. *Capital: A Critique of Political Economy*. Vol. 1. Penguin Classics.
Mason, D. R., and V. A. Beard. 2008. "Community-Based Planning and Poverty Alleviation in Oaxaca, Mexico." *Journal of Planning Education and Research* 27 (3): 245–260.
Matute, I. D. 2021. "Indigeneity as a Transnational Battlefield: Disputes over Meanings, Spaces and Peoples." *Globalizations* 18 (2): 256–272.
Merci Mercado. n.d. Home page. Accessed November 1, 2024. https://mercimercado.com/.
Messer, E. 2007. "Cultural Factors in Food Habits: Reflections in Memory of Christine S. Wilson." *Ecology of Food and Nutrition* 46 (3–4): 185–204.
Mintz, Sidney W. 1985. *Sweetness and Power: The Place of Sugar in Modern History*. Penguin Books.
Mkono, M. 2011. "The Othering of Food in Touristic Eatertainment: A Netnography." *Tourist Studies* 11 (3): 253–270.
Moragues-Faus, A., and T. Marsden. 2017. "The Political Ecology of Food: Carving 'Spaces of Possibility' in a New Research Agenda." *Journal of Rural Studies* 55:275–288.

Murphy, A. D., and H. A. Selby. 1985. "Poverty and the Domestic Cycle in Oaxaca." *Urban Anthropology and Studies of Cultural Systems and World Economic Development* 14 (4): 347–365.

Nigenda, G., E. Orozco, M. Guzmán, G. Mora, L. Lockett, and C. Pacheco. 1998. "The Role of Priority Programmes in the Provision of Health Services in the State of Oaxaca, Mexico." *Health Policy* 43 (2): 125–139.

Nova, C. M. 2003. "The 'Culture' of Exclusion: Representations of Indigenous Women Street Vendors in Tijuana, Mexico." *Bulletin of Latin American Research* 22 (3): 249–268.

Novak, B., and J. A. Hernández Flores. 2022. "A Year and a Half into the Pandemic in Mexico: Evidence of Differences in COVID-19 Mortality Between Indigenous and Non-Indigenous Populations Continues to Accumulate." *Alternative: An International Journal of Indigenous Peoples* 18 (4): 613–624.

Novotny, I. P., P. Tittonell, M. H. Fuentes-Ponce, S. López-Ridaura, and W. A. H. Rossing. 2021. "The Importance of the Traditional Milpa in Food Security and Nutritional Self-Sufficiency in the Highlands of Oaxaca, Mexico." *PLoS One* 16 (2): e0246281.

Núñez-Rocha, G. M., B. M. Esqueda-Eguía, A. M. Salinas-Martínez, et al. 2021. "Differences in Social Determinants of Health Between Urban Indigenous Migrants and Non-Indigenous People in North-Eastern Mexico: An Analysis to Prioritize." *International Journal of Environmental Research and Public Health* 18 (16): 8464.

Oaxaca Auténtico. n.d. "Chapulines: Exotic Food of Ancestral Origin." Accessed April 23, 2024. https://oaxacaautentico.com/en/chapulines-exotic-food-of-ancestral-origin/.

Oaxaca de Juárez. n.d. "Mercado 20 de Noviembre." Accessed October 15, 2024. https://mercado-20-de-noviembre.webnode.mx/.

Oaxaca de mis Amores. n.d. "Chapulines." Accessed November 1, 2023. https://oaxacademisamores.com/products/chapulines (site discontinued).

Ochoa, E. 2000. *Feeding Mexico: The Political Uses of Food Since 1910*. Scholarly Resources.

Olano, M. 2020. "Chapulines, un deleite prehispánico con sabor a Puebla." *Revista La Campiña*, July 17. https://revistalacampina.mx/2020/07/17/chapulines.

Olko, J., A. Galbarczyk, J. Maryniak, et al. 2023. "The Spiral of Disadvantage: Ethnolinguistic Discrimination, Acculturative Stress and Health in Nahua Indigenous Communities in Mexico." *American Journal of Biological Anthropology* 181 (3): 364–378.

Ortega Olivares, M., and F. Mora Rosales. 2014. "Mayordomías y Fiestas Patronales en los Pueblos Originarios de Santa Ana Tlacotenco y Santiago Tzapotitlan, Nahuas del Distrito Federal, México." *Diálogo Andino* 43:51–63.

Ortner, S. B. 1973. "On Key Symbols." *American Anthropologist* 75 (5): 1338–1346.

Otero, G. 2018. *The Neoliberal Diet: Healthy Profits, Unhealthy People*. University of Texas Press.

Pali-Schöll, I., R. Binder, Y. Moens, F. Polesny, and S. Monsó. 2019. "Edible Insects—Defining Knowledge Gaps in Biological and Ethical Considerations of Entomophagy." *Critical Reviews in Food Science and Nutrition* 59 (17): 2760–2771.

Parsons, E. W. C. 1936. *Mitla: Town of the Souls, and Other Zapoteco-Speaking Pueblos of Oaxaca, Mexico*. University of Chicago Press.

Party Bugs. n.d. "What Do Insects Taste Like?" Accessed December 23, 2023. https://www.partybugs.com/en/what-do-edible.
Patil, C. L., and S. L. Young. 2012. "Biocultural Considerations of Food Cravings and Aversions: An Introduction." *Ecology of Food and Nutrition* 51 (5): 365–373.
Payne, C. L. R., and J. Van Itterbeeck. 2017. "Ecosystem Services from Edible Insects in Agricultural Systems: A Review." *Insects* 8 (1): 24.
Pérez-Ferrer, C., A. H. Auchincloss, T. Barrientos-Gutierrez, et al. 2020. "Longitudinal Changes in the Retail Food Environment in Mexico and Their Association with Diabetes." *Health Place* 66:102461.
Pérez-Lloréns, J. L. 2024. "Entomogastronomy, a Step Beyond Just Eating Insects." In *Insects as Food and Food Ingredients*, edited by M. García-Vaquero and C. Álvarez García. Academic Press.
Pérez Rodríguez, V., S. Morell-Hart, and S. M. King, eds. 2024. *Mesquite Pods to Mezcal: 10,000 Years of Oaxacan Cuisines*. University of Texas Press.
Pérez-Tepayo, S., S. Rodríguez-Ramírez, M. Unar-Munguía, and T. Shamah-Levy. 2020. "Trends in the Dietary Patterns of Mexican Adults by Sociodemographic Characteristics." *Nutrition Journal* 19:51.
Peterson, N. D., and A. Freidus. 2023. "University Student Food Insecurity as a Form of Structural Violence." *Human Organization* 82 (2): 182–194.
Pinzón-Pérez, H., and L. V. Santos. 2021. "Comunidades indígenas de Oaxaca, México: Problemas, oportunidades y retos en salud pública con atención especial en salud mental." *Revista de la Facultad de Medicina Humana* 21 (3): 691–698.
Pitrou, P. 2015. "Life as a Process of Making in the Mixe Highlands (Oaxaca, Mexico): Towards a 'General Pragmatics' of Life." *Journal of the Royal Anthropological Institute* 21 (1): 86–105.
Poma, G., M. Cuykx, E. Amato, C. Calaprice, J. F. Focant, and A. Covaci. 2017. "Evaluation of Hazardous Chemicals in Edible Insects and Insect-Based Food Intended for Human Consumption." *Food and Chemical Toxicology* 100:70–79.
Poole, D. 2004. "An Image of 'Our Indian': Type Photographs and Racial Sentiments in Oaxaca, 1920–1940." *Hispanic American Historical Review* 84 (1): 37–82.
Poshadri, A., R. Palthiya, S. Charan G., and P. Butti. 2018. "Insects as an Alternate Source for Food to Conventional Food Animals." *International Journal of Pure and Applied Bioscience* 6 (2): 697–705.
Powis, T. G., E. Gallaga Murrieta, R. Lesure, et al. 2013. "Prehispanic Use of Chili Peppers in Chiapas, Mexico." *PLoS One* 8 (11): e79013.
Proust, M. 1970. *Remembrance of Things Past*. Random House.
Puyana Mutis, A., and C. Márquez Moranchel. 2021. "Discrimination Against Women in Mexico's Three Main Population Groups Integrating Mexican Society." In *Effective Elimination of Structural Racism*. Edited by E. Guerrero. IntechOpen.
Ramírez-Arriaga, E., L. A. Navarro-Calvo, and E. Díaz-Carbajal. 2011. "Botanical Characterisation of Mexican Honeys from a Subtropical Region (Oaxaca) Based on Pollen Analysis." *Grana* 50 (1): 40–54.
Ramos, M. E., D. E. Gibaja-Romero, and S. A. Ochoa. 2020. "Gender Inequality and Gender-Based Poverty in Mexico." *Heliyon* 6 (1): e03322.
Ramos-Elorduy, J. 1997. "The Importance of Edible Insects in the Nutrition and Economy of People of the Rural Areas of Mexico." *Ecology of Food and Nutrition* 36 (5): 347–366.

Ramos-Elorduy, J. 2002. "Edible Insects of Chiapas, Mexico." *Ecology of Food and Nutrition* 41 (4): 271–299.
Ramos-Elorduy, J. 2009. "Anthropo-Entomophagy: Cultures, Evolution and Sustainability." *Entomological Research* 39 (5): 271–288.
Ramos-García, J. L., D. Vargas-Chanes, and A. Toledo-López. 2023. "Perception of Social Prosperity in Indigenous Tourism Destinations in Mexico: The Mediator Effect of Competitiveness of the Destinations." *Cogent Business and Management* 10 (2): 2235105.
Reguart, M. 2021. "Telecommunication Regulatory Policy and the Effect of Institutions on Competition, Access, and Adoption of Broadband Internet Services in Mexico, 2013–2018." *International Journal of Technology, Knowledge, and Society* 17 (1): 1–18.
Robles García, N. M. 2024. "Itacate para el Camino: Prepared Meals for Prehispanic and Colonial Travelers." In *Mesquite Pods to Mezcal: 10,000 Years of Oaxacan Cuisines*, edited by V. Pérez Rodríguez, S. Morell-Hart, and S. M. King. University of Texas Press.
Rudra, N., and J. Tobin. 2017. "When Does Globalization Help the Poor?" *Annual Review of Political Science* 20:287–307.
Ruiz, A., C. Altesor, and E. Olvera. 2021. *The Food of Oaxaca: Recipes and Stories from Mexico's Culinary Capital: A Cookbook*. Knopf Doubleday.
Sada, A. 2013. "Explainer: Mexico's 2013 Reforms." Americas Society/Council of the Americas, December 17. https://www.as-coa.org/articles/explainer-mexicos-2013-reforms.
Salinas, J. J., S. Al Snih, K. Markides, L. A. Ray, and R. J. Angel. 2010. "The Rural-Urban Divide: Health Services Utilization Among Older Mexicans in Mexico." *Journal of Rural Health* 26 (4): 333–341.
Sammells, C. A. 2019. "Reimagining Bolivian Cuisine: Haute Traditional Food and Its Discontents." *Food and Foodways* 27 (4): 338–352.
Sammells, C. A. 2024. "Cooking in the Past and for the Future in Latin America." *Latin American Research Review* 59 (2): 1–14.
Samson, M. 1995. "Towards a 'Friday' Model of International Trade: A Feminist Deconstruction of Race and Gender Bias in the Robinson Crusoe Trade Allegory." *Canadian Journal of Economics / Revue canadienne d'Economique* 28 (1): 143–158.
Secretaría de Gobernación. 2020. "Acuerdo por el que se declara como emergencia sanitaria por causa de fuerza mayor, a la epidemia de enfermedad generada por el virus SARS-CoV2 (COVID-19)." Diario Oficial de la Federación, March 30. https://www.dof.gob.mx/nota_detalle.php?codigo=5590745.
Serpico, M., D. Rovai, K. Wilke, R. Lesniauskas, J. Garza, and A. Lammert. 2021. "Studying the Emotional Response to Insects Food Products." *Foods* 10 (10): 2404.
Servan-Mori, E., P. Torres-Pereda, E. Orozco, and S. G. Sosa-Rubí. 2014. "An Explanatory Analysis of Economic and Health Inequality Changes Among Mexican Indigenous People, 2000–2010." *International Journal of Equity Health* 13:21.
Silva, S. 2024. "Espejismo Oaxaqueño." *Medium*, March 27. https://medium.com/@ssilva1979/espejismo-oaxaque-d2967fb0f26b.
Smith, B. C. 2016. "Proust, the Madeleine and Memory." In *Memory in the Twenty-First Century: New Critical Perspectives from the Arts, Humanities, and Sciences*, edited by S. Groes. Palgrave Macmillan.

Smyth, A. 2022. "Challenging the Financialization of Remittances Agenda Through Indigenous Women's Practices in Oaxaca." *Environment and Planning A: Economy and Space* 54 (4): 761–778.
Smyth, A. 2024. "Making Futures in Oaxaca: Remittances in the Diverse Economies of Social Reproduction." *Transactions of the Institute of British Geographers* 49 (2): e12659.
Soleri, D., D. A. Cleveland, and F. Aragón Cuevas. 2008. "Food Globalization and Local Diversity: The Case of Tejate." *Current Anthropology* 49 (2): 281–290.
Soleri, D., D. A. Cleveland, F. Aragón Cuevas, V. Jimenez, and M. C. Wang. 2023. "Traditional Foods, Globalization, Migration, and Public and Planetary Health: The Case of Tejate, a Maize and Cacao Beverage in Oaxacalifornia." *Challenges* 14 (1): 9.
Song, H., R. Mariño-Pérez, D. A. Woller, and M. M. Cigliano. 2018. "Evolution, Diversification, and Biogeography of Grasshoppers (Orthoptera: Acrididae)." *Insect Systematics and Diversity* 2 (4): 3.
Spence, C. 2021. "Explaining Seasonal Patterns of Food Consumption." *International Journal of Gastronomy and Food Science* 24:100332.
Spotify. n.d. "Chapulines." Accessed June 10, 2024. https://open.spotify.com/artist/4RYWK04ecJyOoL4VrZKMbi.
Staller, J. E., and M. Carrasco. 2010. *Pre-Columbian Foodways: Interdisciplinary Approaches to Food, Culture, and Markets in Ancient Mesoamerica*. Springer.
Statista. 2024. "Average Monthly Wages in Oaxaca from 2010 to 2023." Updated July 5. https://www.statista.com/statistics/1390264/.
Stephen, L. 1991. *Zapotec Women*. University of Texas Press.
Suzuki, Y., T. Narumi, T. Tanikawa, and M. Hirose. 2021. "Taste in Motion: The Effect of Projection Mapping of a Boiling Effect on Food Expectation, Food Perception, and Purchasing Behavior." *Frontiers in Computer Science* 3:662824.
Svanberg, I., and Å. Berggren. 2021. "Insects as Past and Future Food in Entomophobic Europe." *Food, Culture and Society* 24 (5): 624–638.
Tomassini, L., S. Staffieri, and E. Cavagnaro. 2021. "Local Food Consumption and Practice Theory: A Case Study on Guests' Motivations and Understanding." *Research in Hospitality Management* 11 (2): 93–100.
Tumbaga, A. Z. 2020. "Indios y burros: Rethinking 'la India María' as Ethnographic Cinema." *Latin American Research Review* 55 (4): 759–772.
Vaccaro, I., and E. Ortiz Díaz. 2021. "The Effects of Migration on Peasant Agricultural Systems: Oaxacan Villages, Between Remittances and Market Integration." *Culture, Agriculture, Food and Environment* 43 (1): 47–59.
Valerino-Perea, S., L. Lara-Castor, M. E. G. Armstrong, and A. Papadaki. 2019. "Definition of the Traditional Mexican Diet and Its Role in Health: A Systematic Review." *Nutrients* 11 (11): 2803.
van Bavel, B., and M. Scheffer. 2021. "Historical Effects of Shocks on Inequality: The Great Leveler Revisited." *Humanities and Social Sciences Communications* 8:76.
van Huis, A. 2017. "Did Early Humans Consume Insects?" *Journal of Insects as Food and Feed* 3 (3): 161–163.
van Huis, A., A. Halloran, J. Van Itterbeeck, H. Klunder, and Y. Vantomme. 2022. "How Many People on Our Planet Eat Insects: 2 Billion?" *Journal of Insects as Food and Feed* 8 (1): 1–4.

van Huis, A., J. Van Itterbeeck, H. Klunder, et al. 2013. *Edible Insects: Future Prospects for Food and Feed Security*. Food and Agriculture Organization of the United Nations.
Venancio-Guzmán, S., A. I. Aguirre-Salado, C. Soubervielle-Montalvo, and J. d. C. Jiménez-Hernández. 2022. "Assessing the Nationwide COVID-19 Risk in Mexico Through the Lens of Comorbidity by an XGBoost-Based Logistic Regression Model." *International Journal of Environmental Research and Public Health* 19 (19): 11992.
Villalobos Portilla, E. 2024. "Normalization of Social Inequality and Its Implications: The Case of Zaachila Oriente in Oaxaca." PhD diss., Humboldt-Universität zu Berlin.
von Bremzen, A. 2023. *National Dish: Around the World in Search of Food, History, and the Meaning of Home*. Penguin Press.
Wade, M. 2021. "Gateway Bugs: Disgust in Food System Pedagogy." *Sensorium*. Culture & Agriculture, American Anthropological Association, April 21. https://www.cultureandagriculture.org/sensorium/gateway-bugs-disgust-in-food-system-pedagogy.
Warde, A. 2016. *The Practice of Eating*. Polity Press.
Weslander, L. 2019. "The Culinary Tradition Behind Chapulines: Oaxaca's Fried Grasshoppers." Travel Awaits, September 19. https://www.travelawaits.com/2479558/.
Whitford, M. 2009. "Oaxaca's Indigenous Guelaguetza Festival: Not All That Glistens Is Gold." *Event Management* 12 (3–4): 143–161.
Wilk, R. 2004. "Morals and Metaphors: The Meaning of Consumption." In *Elusive Consumption*, edited by K. Eckstron and H. Brembeck. Berg.
Wilk, R. 2006. *Home Cooking in the Global Village: Caribbean Food from Buccaneers to Ecotourists*. Bloomsbury.
Wilson, T. D. 2008. "Economic and Social Impacts of Tourism in Mexico." *Latin American Perspectives* 35 (3): 37–52.
World Bank. n.d. "Poverty." Accessed June 10, 2024. https://www.worldbank.org/en/topic/poverty.
Worthen, H. 2015. "Indigenous Women's Political Participation: Gendered Labor and Collective Rights Paradigms in Mexico." *Gender and Society* 29 (6): 914–936.
Wylie, L. 2006. "Colonial Tropes and Postcolonial Tricks: Rewriting the Tropics in the 'Novela de la selva.'" *Modern Language Review* 101 (3): 728–742.
Yamagishi, T., Y. Li, H. Takagishi, Y. Matsumoto, and T. Kiyonari. 2014. "In Search of *Homo economicus*." *Psychological Science* 25 (9): 1699–1711.
Yen, A. L. 2015. "Insects as Food and Feed in the Asia Pacific Region: Current Perspectives and Future Directions." *Journal of Insects as Food and Feed* 1 (1): 33–55.
Young, F. W., D. K. Freebairn, and R. Snipper. 1979. "The Structural Context of Rural Poverty in Mexico: A Cross-State Comparison." *Economic Development and Cultural Change* 27 (4): 669–686.
Youssef, J., and C. Spence. 2021. "Introducing Diners to the Range of Experiences in Creative Mexican Cuisine, Including the Consumption of Insects." *International Journal of Gastronomy and Food Science* 25 (12): 100371.
YouTube. n.d. "Chapulines Son." Accessed June 10, 2024. https://www.youtube.com/@ChapulinesSon/featured.

INDEX

Note: *Italicized* page references indicate table, figure, or photo.

abuse, 34, 100
Afro-Caribbeans, 77
ahuatle (water bug eggs), 3
alcoholism, 97
Alebrijes, 5
alfalfa: chapulines in fields of, 1, 10, 14, 37, 39, 112; nymphs in, 40, 41
alfalfaros (alfalfa farmers), 42
Altamirano, Rosa, 81
amarga. See bitter
ambulantes (street venders), 90, 124n2
ant eggs (*escamoles*), 3, 57
anthropology: chapulineras and, xiii; on entomophagy, 14; on Indigenous peoples, 10
Armelagos, George J., 14–15
artesanos (craftspeople), 82, 93, *94*
astaxanthin, 45
asthma, 22, 29
atole, 60
Avendaño, Columba, 56, 57
axayacatl (water bugs), 57
Azaria, Isahrai, 123n3, 124n6
Aztecs, 23

babies (*nenes*), 40
bakery (*pandadería*), *54*
Baptista, Sofia, 41, 42–43
beans, 57, *59*, 60, 65
beef, 3, 23; hamburgers, 49, 56; overreliance on, 13; *tasajo frito*, 56
bigotry, 85
bitter (*amarga*), 40; crickets as, 55
black mole (*mole negro*), 60–61
blights, 24

boiling, of chapulines, 39, 45, *46*
Borgen Project, 122n5
Brachystola magna (plains lubber grasshoppers), 92
breads, 25, 57, 59
Brillat-Savarin, Jean Anthelme, 78
broth/soup (*caldo*), 49, 60

calcium, 63; in COVID-19 pandemic, 107
caldo (broth/soup), 49, 60
Canedo, Ana, 31
Carrasco, Michael, 76
casta system, 23–34
cattle, 14, 64. *See also* beef
cazuela, 45
celebrations: chapulines in, 5; in COVID-19 pandemic, 103; Day of the Dead, xii, 82; Food of the Gods Festival, 124n4; Guelaguetza, 82; *mayordomías*, 103
cell phones, 99–100
cempasúchiles (marigolds), xii, xiii
Centro de Abastos, xii, *21*, 81, 93
Cerritos-Flores, Rene, 29
chapulin, xiv, 7, 68, 75
chapulineras, 1–15, *2*, 19–35, *21*, *62*; abundance of, 40; adaptability of, 109; age of, 27, 28; anthropology and, xiii; bakery of, *54*; challenges of, 20–22, 70, 104; contracts with, 85; in COVID-19 pandemic, 95–105, 110, 114; education of, 20, 21, 28–29, 122n5; entrepreneurship of, 22, 30, 32, 87–88, *88*, 89, 90–91, *91*, 93,

110, *114*; as family providers, 87, *88*, 90, *91*, 108; harvesting/harvesters and, 40, 83–85, 91; health-care expenses of, 21–22, 29; hometowns of, 26–27, *27*; hope of, 34–35; idealized vision of, 73; as ignored and overlooked, 4; income of, 10–11, 20, 90–92; independence of, 28; as local retailers, 87–89, *88*, *91*, *94*; marginality of, 32–35, *34*; marital status of, 28; marketing by, 13–15, 81–95, *94*, 109–110; mistrust by, 86–87; negotiation by, 30, 86; NGOs and, 9, 22, 86; in part-time employment, 30; poverty of, 72; pseudonyms for, 121; in racialized and gender economic system, 21; in restaurant, *39*; sales control of, 73, *73*; shipping by, 112; as street venders, 90, 124n2; as unused term, 121n1; as wholesalers, *88*, 89–90, *91*, 93. *See also specific topics*
Chapulineros, Los, 69
chapulines: in advertising and promotion, 69–70; age and maturity of, 42; availability of, 8–9; boiling of, 39, 45, *46*; in celebrations, 5; changes to, 8; color red of, 45, *46*; cost of, 61, 84; eating, 46–50, 53–64; egg hatchings and molts of, 40; experience of, 65–78; frying of, 54; growth cycle of, 55, 83; harvesting of, 9–10, 37–45, 83–85, *91*, *92*; Indigenous peoples and, 2–8, 107, 112; inequality and, 21, 23, 74, 109, 111; jumping speed of, 42; lead in, 3, 107, 113, 121n3; as logos, 68; meaning for, 12, 69; nutrients in, 63; nymphs of, 40, 41, 42; outsiders and, 72–73, 77, 86–87; pesticides in, 25, 43, 70, 107, 113; as plague, 84; poverty and, 20, 21, 31, 48, 107, 111; in pre-Columbia, 3–4, 6–8, 67, 107, 112; protein from, 5–6, 8, 14, 25, 47–48, 63, 103, 108, 124n5; resting of, 44–45; sales to outsiders, 4–8, 29–30, 47–48; sales volume of, 29, 87–89, *88*; sautée of, 63; seasonality, xiii, 6, 57, 58, 61, 72, 85, 93; should we be eating them, 107–115; sorting and cleaning of, 39, 42, 43–44; Spain and, 24; spirituality of, 67, 68, 75, 108; spoiling of, 44; sustainability of, 68, 69, 108, 112; symbolism of, 5, 8–9, 68–69, 74, 77–78, 109, 112; taste of, xiii–xiv; toasting of, 39, 45; total weight living on crops and, 29, 84; tourists and, 8–9; uniformity of, 43–44; wholesale cost of, 84. *See also specific topics*
Chapulines en Venta, *62*, 81–82, 103
Chapulines Oaxaqueños, 81–82, 103
cheese, 55, 56; in *chile rellenos*, 63; in pasta, 62; sales by chapulineras, 93
chicatanas (water bugs), xiii, 3, 30, 57, 93, 94
chicken, 47, 60; in pasta, 62
children, 28, 86, 111, 114; in college, xi, 115; in COVID-19 pandemic, 96; diet of, 59–60, 63; education of, 22, 122n5; harvesting by, 37–38, 40, 43; marginality of, 32–33; pizza and, 56, 60; ultra-processed foods and, 63
chile rellenos, 63
chiles, 44, 45, 46, 57; in *huevos a la Mexicana*, 60; in pasta, 62
chocolate, 55, 59, 61, 67, 123n3
climate change, 13, 70; entomophagy and, 115
coffee, 60
college, children in, xi, 115
comal (cooking grill), 6, 39, 45, 112
comfort food, 12
comida de la chatarra (junk food), 56
communal fields, 40, 83, 91, *92*
CONAPO. *See* Consejo Nacional de Poblacion
Consejo Nacional de Ciencia y Tecnologia (National Council of Science and Technology), 96
Consejo Nacional de Poblacion (CONAPO, National Population Council of Mexico), 32
Conservatory of the Mexican Gastronomic Culture, 124n8
contracts, with chapulineras, 85
cookbooks, 6, 122n6
cooking grill (*comal*), 6, 39, 45, 112
corn. *See maíz*
corn flakes, 49

COVID-19 pandemic, 5, 8, 10, 13; calcium in, 107; chapulineras in, 95–105, 110, 114; health-care expenses in, 22, 29; health care in, 96; infection cases in, 124n1; iron in, 107; kitchen gardens in, 57; marginality in, 34; protein in, 107; research and programming in, 122n3
craftspeople (*artesanos*), 82, 93, *94*
crema de chapulines, 123n2
crickets, 7, 55
crisis food, 5, 12–13
crop failures, 47
crustacyanin, 45
Culinary Backstreets, 14

dare foods, of tourists, 49–50, 71, 121n7
Day of the Dead (Dia de los Muertos), xii, 82
depression, 22; marginality and, 32
diabetes, 22, 29, 123n2; in COVID-19 pandemic, 97; rate of, 123n6
Dia de los Muertos (Day of the Dead), xii, 82
Díaz, Daniela Aquino, 98–99
discrimination, 34, 70; in COVID-19 pandemic, 97; outsiders and, 72, 74; from Spanish, 77; toward chapulineras, 85
drought, 5, 8, 24, 47

Earle, Rebecca, 24
earthquakes, 8, 47
education, 77; of chapulineras, 20, 21, 28–29, 122n5; of children, 22, 122n5; of Indigenous peoples, 34; marginality and, 32
eggs: ant, 3, 57; in *huevos a la Mexicana*, 60
El Chapulín Colorado, 121n5
electricity, 32, 58–59
elote, 60
Endfield, Georgina, 24
entomophagy, 3, 6; anthropology on, 14; climate change and, 115; as common in Mexico, xiv; global consumption of, 12; Indigenous peoples and, 107–108; marginality and, 107–108; in Mexican Revolution, 24; omnivores and, 11; poverty and, 107–108; in pre-Columbia, xiv, 22–23; protein from, 11
entomophobia, 11, 55, 66
entrepreneurship, of chapulineras, 22, 30, 32, 87–88, *88*, *89*, 90–91, *91*, 93, 110, *114*
escamoles (ant eggs), 3, 57
exports, 13–14, 29

Facebook, 81–82; in COVID-19 pandemic, 101–102, 103
family providers, chapulineras as, 87, *88*, 90, *91*, 108
famine, 13
Federal Law on the Protection of Personal Data Held by Private Parties, 125n2
Federal Telecommunications Law, 101
fetishizing, 67, 68, 70–71, 72, 77, 78
financial services, 125n3
floods, 24
foodies, 6, 8, 9, 47, 48, 123n3; co-opting local traditions by, 15; experience of, 65–78; pre-Columbia and, 112
food insecurity, 57, 70, 74
food of the gods, 67, 68, 70–71, 74, 112
Food of the Gods Festival, 124n4
foodways, 76
freeze-drying, 83
FTD Travel, 124n4
Fuentes, Natalia, 98

gag reflex, 75
Gálvez, Alyshia, 9
Garcia, Amanda, 62
Garcia, Minerva, 94
Garcia, Miriam, 111
gardens: kitchen, 56–57. *See also* milpas
garlic, 44, 45, 46, 63
gender stereotypes/bias, 34, 105; cell phones and, 100
globalization, 113
Gómez Bolaños, Roberto, 121n5
Gonzalez, Adriana Soledad, 58
grasshoppers (*Saltamontes*), 7; as plagues, 25, 122n2; tourists and, 30; in Triassic period, 10–11. *See also* chapulines
greenhouse gases, 13

Greenwald, Rebecca, 123n3
grillos, 55
Guatemala, 77
Guelaguetza, 82
gusanos (worms or larvae), xiii, 3
Gutiérrez-Zamora, Violeta, 86
Guzma, Paola, 1, 101

hamburgers, 49, 56
harvesting/harvesters, of chapulines, 9–10, 37–45, *91, 92*; chapulineras and, 40, 83–85, 91; by children, 37–38, 40, 43; in milpas, 40–41, 91; of nymphs, 41
health care, 77; in COVID-19 pandemic, 96; marginality and, 32
health-care expenses: of chapulineras, 21–22, 29; in COVID-19 pandemic, 97, 102
heavy metals, 113
Hererra, Catalina, 98
Hernandez, Maria, 42
huertas familiares (kitchen gardens), 56–57
Hipolito, Ivanna, 53, 54–55, 59–60
Historia general de las cosas de Nueva España (Sahagún), 23
Honduras, 77
hot dogs, 60
huevos a la Mexicana, 60
hypertension, 22, 29; in COVID-19 pandemic, 97

İlda, Mehmet Murat, 39
illiteracy, 32
Indigenous peoples: chapulines and, 2–8, 107, 112; education of, 34; marginality of, 32; outsiders on, 76; poverty of, 31–32, 33, 58–59, 70; tortillas and, 113; as typically victims of progress, 10. *See also* chapulineras
inequality, 58, 66, 70, 122n1; in *casta* system, 23–34; chapulineras and, 21, 109; chapulines and, 74, 111; in COVID-19 pandemic, 97; outsiders and, 72, 74
Instituto Nacional de Estadistica y Geografia (INEGI, National Institute of Statistics and Geography), 32

iron, 63; in COVID-19 pandemic, 107; deficiency of, 56
Ítaka, María, 14

jumiles (stink bugs), 3
junk food (*comida de la chatarra*), 56

kitchen gardens (*huertas familiares*), 56–57
Krieger, Nat, 65

lead, 3, 107, 113, 121n3
lemon juice, 45
Lévi-Strauss, Claude, 66–67
limón (lime), 39, 45, 46, 47; in pasta, 62
local retailers, chapulineras as, 87–89, *88, 91, 94*
logos, chapulines as, 68
Lopez, Elena, 55
Luxury Wanderer, 123n2

madeleine, 111
maíz (corn): chapuline damage to, 84; chapulines in fields of, 1, 37, 39, 40, 41, 60, 112; importance in diet, 57–58. *See also* tortillas
marginality: of chapulineras, 32–35, *34*; chapulines and, 107–108; in COVID-19 pandemic, 34, 97; *maíz* and, 57; outsiders and, 72
marigolds (*cempasúchiles*), xii, xiii
Martinez, Carla, 19, 29, 53
más dulce (sweeter), 40
Mauro, Don, xii
mayordomías, 103
meat, 57, 59, 96; in COVID-19 pandemic, 103. *See also* beef
Melcho, Olivia, 1
Mendoza, Carmen, 37, 47, 95
mental health, 22
El Mercado de la Merced, xii
Merci Mercado, 123n2
mestiza, 72
Mexican Revolution, 8, 19, 24–25, 47; entomophagy in, 24
mezcal, xiv, 4, 9, 49, 66, 67, 82; for tourists, 115
mezcaleros, 82
microwave ovens, 58–59

Middle Easterners, 77
milpas (gardens), 10, 83; harvesting in, 40–41, 91
minimum wage, 32, 123n7
Mintz, Sidney W., 110
Mixe, 69, 122n4
Mixtec, 69, 123n3
molcajete (mortar and pestle), 62
mole, 3, 4, 67; sales by chapulineras, 93
mole amarillo (yellow mole), 60
mole negro (black mole), 60–61
Morales, Petrona, 49
Moreno, Genevieve, 59
mortar and pestle (*molcajete*), 62
Munoz, Lorena, 56, 63
"Myths, Molinillos, and Maps" (Azaria), 123n3

NAFTA. *See* North American Free Trade Agreement
National Council of Science and Technology (Consejo Nacional de Ciencia y Tecnologia), 96
National Institute of Statistics and Geography. *See* Instituto Nacional de Estadistica y Geografia
National Population Council for Mexico. *See* Consejo Nacional de Poblacion
NEGI. *See* Instituto Nacional de Estadistica y Geografia
nenes (babies), 40
NGOs, 9, 22, 86
Nicaragua, 77
North American Free Trade Agreement (NAFTA), xiv, 9
nymphs, 40; harvesting of, 41; higher price for, 42

Oaxaca de mis Amores, 124n9
obesity, 22, 29, 123n2
Ochoa, Enrique, 25
omnivores, 11
onions, 47, 54, 57, 63; in *huevos a la Mexicana*, 60
out-migration, 110–111
outsiders: chapulineras and, 77, 86–87; fetishizing by, 67, 68, 70–71, 72, 77, 78; on Indigenous peoples, 76;

marketing to, 83; pre-Columbia and, 112; sale of chapulines to, 4–8, 29–30, 47–48. *See also* foodies; tourists

packaged foods, 56
painted (*pintado*), 93
pandadería (bakery), 54
Parsons, Elsie Clews, xiv
Party Bugs, 123n1
pasta, 62
peanuts, 30, 94
peppers (*rajas*), 54
Pérez, Reyna, 60, 61–62
pesticides: in chapulines, 25, 43, 70, 107, 113; for plagues, 92
pintado (painted), 93
pizza, 56, 60
plagues, 92; chapulines as, 84; grasshoppers as, 25, 122n2
plains lubber grasshoppers (*Brachystola magna*), 92
post-traumatic stress disorder, 32
poverty, 20, 21, 48, 107–108, 111; of chapulineras, 72; in COVID-19 pandemic, 97; defined, 123n8; of Indigenous peoples, 31–32, 33, 58–59, 70; marginality and, 32
pragmatic political economy, 110
pre-Columbia: chapulines in, 3–8, 67, 107, 112; entomophagy in, xiv, 22–23
protein: from chapulines, 5–6, 8, 14, 25, 47–48, 63, 103, 108, 124n5; in COVID-19 pandemic, 103, 107; from entomophagy, 11; from Spain, 11, 113
Proust, Marcel, 111

quesillo: in pasta, 62; sales by chapulineras, 93
queso fresco, 93

rajas (peppers), 54
ramen (*soup maruchan*), 56
Ramirez, Julian, 44–45, 85
ready-made foods, 56, 57–58, 123n2
refrigerators, 58–59, 61
Reyes, Miranda, 38–39, 41, 115
rice, 47, 57, 60; in *chile rellenos*, 63
Rodríquez, Eugenia, 53

Ruiz, Adriana, 81, 82
Ruiz, Fernanda, 95

SADER. *See* Secretaria de Agricultura y Desarrollo Rural
Sahagún, Bernardino de, 23
sal de gusano, xiii, 30, 44, 45, 46, 47; sales by chapulineras, 93, *94*
salsa, 47, 55, 63, 66; in *huevos a la Mexicana*, 60
salt, 45
Saltamontes. *See* grasshoppers
seasonality, chapulines, xiii, 6, 57, 58, 61, 72, 85, 93
Secretaria de Agricultura y Desarrollo Rural (SADER), 25, 92, 122n2
Sierra Mixe, 122n4
Silva, Teresa, 37, 47
soccer team, 69
social media, 13–14, 81–82, 122n6; in COVID-19 pandemic, 101–103
sopa de guías, 58
soup maruchan (ramen), 56
Spain/Spanish, 4, 19; *casta* system of, 24; chapulines and, 24; discrimination from, 77; non-native animals and crops from, 23; protein of, 11, 113; violence of, 77, 124n6
spirituality, 67, 68, 75, 108
squash, 57
Staller, John Edward, 76
stink bugs (*jumiles*), 3
stoves, 58–59, 61
street venders (*ambulantes*), 90, 124n2
structural inequality, 4, 26, 58, 109–110
structural poverty, 59
sugar, 110
sustainability, 68, 69, 108, 112
sweeter (*más dulce*), 40
Sweetness and Power (Mintz), 110

tacos, 7, 39, 55
tamales, 60, 73
tapetes (woolen rugs), xi
tasajo frito (thin, dried beef), 56
toasting, of chapulines, 39, 45
tomatillos, 47
tomatoes, 57
tortillas, 3, 11, 25, 47, 49, 55, 57, 66; fire pit for, 58; Indigenous peoples and, 113; with pasta, 62; sales by chapulineras, 93
totems, 66–67
touchless economy, in COVID-19 pandemic, 101, 104–105, 122n3
tourists, 6, 48; bonus sales to, 30; challenges of growth of, 123n3; chapulineras and, 8–9; after COVID-19 pandemic, 104; dare foods of, 49–50, 71, 121n7; experience of, 65–78; marketing to, 82; mezcal for, 115; pre-Columbia and, 112; rising number of, 15
Triassic period, grasshoppers in, 10–11

ultra-processed foods, 57–58, 123n2; children and, 63
undocumented migrants, 77

Valeriano, Elisa, 99
Valerino-Perea, Selene, 57
vegetables, xii, 48; in *huertas familiares*, 56; sales by chapulineras, 30, 93, *94*
Velsasco, Magdalena, 40–41
violence, 47; of Spanish, 77, 124n6
vitamin A, 63
vitamin C, 63

Warde, Alan, 5
water bug eggs (*ahuatle*), 3
water bugs (*axayacatl*), 57
water bugs (*chicatanas*), xiii, 3, 30, 57, 93, 94
Weslander, Liz, 65, 124n5
WhatsApp, 101–103
wheat, 14, 39
wholesalers: chapulineras as, *88*, 89–90, *91*, 93; cost of, 84
Wilk, Richard, 5
woolen rugs (*tapetes*), xi
World Bank, 123n8
worms or larvae (*gusanos*), xiii, 3

yellow mole (*mole amarillo*), 60
yerba santa, 62

Zapotec, xi–xii, 25–26, 41, 63, 69, 123n3
zinc, 63

www.ingramcontent.com/pod-product-compliance
Lightning Source LLC
Jackson TN
JSHW021256100426
100637JS00002B/8